FEAR

Also by Osho

FEAR

UNDERSTANDING AND ACCEPTING
THE INSECURITIES OF LIFE

Osho

St. Martin's Griffin
New York

Contents

FEAR

Go into your fear.
Silently enter into it, so you can find its depth.
And sometimes it happens that it is not very deep.

A ZEN STORY IS:

A man walking in the night slipped and fell from a rocky path. Afraid he
would fall down thousands of feet, because he knew that just at the edge
of the path was a very deep valley, he grabbed hold of a branch that was
overhanging the edge. In the darkness of night all he could see below him
was a bottomless abyss. He shouted and his own shout was reflected
back—there was nobody to hear him.

You can imagine that man, and his whole night of torture. Every
moment there was death below, his hands were becoming cold, he was losing
his grip . . . but he managed to hold on, and as the sun came out he
looked down . . . and he laughed! There was no abyss. Just six inches
below his feet there was a rock ledge. He could have rested the whole
night, slept well—the ledge was big enough—but instead, the
whole night was a nightmare.

From my own experience I can say to you:
The fear is not more than six inches deep. Now it is up to you whether you
want to go on clinging to the branch and turn your life into a nightmare, or
whether you would love to leave the branch and stand on your feet.

There is nothing to fear.

—OSHO

1

UNDERSTANDING FEAR ITSELF

Fear is as nonsubstantial as your shadow, but it is. The shadow also exists—nonsubstantial, negative, but not nonexistential—and sometimes the shadow can have a great impact on you. In a jungle when the night is approaching you can be frightened of your own shadow. In a lonely place, on a lonely path, you can start running because of your own shadow. Your running will be real, your escaping will be real, but the cause will be nonsubstantial.

You can run away from a rope thinking that it is a snake; if you come back and you look closely and you observe, you will laugh at the whole stupidity of it. But people are afraid to come to places where fear exists. People are more afraid of fear than of anything else, because the very existence of fear shakes your foundations.

The shaking of the foundations is very real, remember. The fear is like a dream, a nightmare, but after a nightmare when you are awake the aftereffects still persist, the hangover persists. Your breathing has changed, you are perspiring, your body is still trembling, you are hot. Now you know that it was just a nightmare, a dream, nonsubstantial, but even this knowing will take time to penetrate to the very core of your being. Meanwhile the effect of the nonsubstantial dream will continue. Fear is a nightmare.

What is fear made of? Fear is made of ignorance of one's own self. There is only one fear; it manifests in many ways, a thousand and one can be the manifestations, but basically fear is one, and that is that "Deep inside, I may not be." And in a way it is true that you are not. Godliness is, you are not. The host is not, the guest is. And because you are suspicious—and your suspicion is valid—you don't look in. You go on pretending that you are; you know that if you look in, you are not! This is a deep, tacit understanding. It is not intellectual, it is existential; it is in your very guts, the feeling that "I may not be. It is better not to look in. Go on looking out." At least it keeps you fooled, it keeps the illusion intact that "I am." But because this feeling of "I amness" is false, it creates fear. You know that anything can destroy it, any deep encounter can shatter it. It can be shattered by love, it can be shattered by a serious disease, it can be shattered by seeing someone die. It can be shattered in many ways, it is very fragile. You are managing it somehow by not looking in.

> *Mulla Nasruddin was traveling on a train. The ticket collector came; he asked for the ticket. He looked in all his pockets, in all his suitcases, and the ticket was not found. He was perspiring, and he was becoming more and more frightened. And then the ticket collector said, "Sir, but you have not looked in one of your pockets. Why don't you look in it?"*

Mulla Nasruddin said, "Please don't talk about that pocket. I am not going to look in it. That is my only hope! If I look in that pocket and it is not found, then it is lost, then it is absolutely not anywhere to be found. I cannot look in that pocket. Mind you, I will look everywhere else; that pocket is my safety, I can still hope that it may be in that pocket. I have left it deliberately and I am not going to touch it. Whether I find the ticket or not, I am not going to look in that particular pocket."

This is the situation with the ego too. You don't look in, that is your only hope: "Who knows? Maybe it is there." But if you look, your intuitive feeling says it is not there.

This false ego, which you have created by not looking in, by continuously looking out, is the root cause of fear. You will be afraid of all those spaces in which you have to look. You will be afraid of beauty because beauty simply throws you within. A beautiful sunset, and all those luminous colors in the clouds, and you will be afraid to look at it because such great beauty is bound to throw you inside yourself. Such great beauty stops your thinking: For a moment the mind is in such awe, it forgets how to think, how to go on spinning and weaving. The inner talk comes to a stop, a halt, and you are suddenly in.

People are afraid of great music, people are afraid of great poetry, people are afraid of deep intimacy. People's love affairs are just hit-and-run affairs. They don't go deep into each other's being because going deep into each other's being, the fear is there—the other's pool of being will reflect you. In that pool, in that mirror of the other's being, if you are not found, if the mirror remains empty, if it reflects nothing, then what?

People are afraid of love. They only pretend, they only go on playing games in the name of love. They are afraid of meditation; even in the name of meditation at the most they go on practicing new ways of thinking. That's what Maharishi Mahesh Yogi's Transcendental Meditation is—it is neither meditation nor transcendental, it is simply chanting a mantra. And chanting a mantra is nothing but a process of thought, concentrated thought. It is again a new device, a device not to meditate. People are repeating Christian prayers, Mohammedan prayers, Hindu prayers—all ways to avoid meditation. These are not meditations, remember. Mind is so cunning that in the name of meditation it has created many false phenomena.

Meditation is when you are not doing anything at all, when the mind is not functioning at all. That nonfunctioning of the mind is meditation—no chanting, no mantra, no image, no concentration. One just simply is. In that isness, the ego disappears, and with the ego the shadow of the ego disappears.

That shadow is fear.

Fear is one of the most important problems. Each human being has to go through it and has to come to a certain understanding about it. The ego gives you the fear that one day you may have to die. You go on deceiving yourself that death happens only to others, and in a way you are right: Some neighbor dies, some acquaintance dies, some friend dies, your wife dies, your mother dies—it always happens to somebody else, never to you. You can hide behind this fact. Maybe you are an exception, you are not going to die. The ego is trying to protect you.

But each time somebody dies, something in you becomes shaky. Each death is a small death to you. Never send somebody to ask for whom the bell tolls, it tolls for thee. Each death is your death. Even when a dry leaf falls from the tree, it is your death. Hence we go on protecting ourselves.

Somebody is dying and we talk about the immortality of the soul, and the leaf is falling from the tree and we say, "Nothing to be worried about. Soon the spring will come and the tree will again have foliage. This is only a change, only the garments are being changed."

People believe in the immortality of the soul not because they *know* but because they are afraid. The more cowardly a person is the more is the possibility that he will believe in the immortality of the soul—not that he is religious, he is simply cowardly. The belief in the immortality of the soul has nothing to do with religion. The religious person knows that "I am not," and then whatever is left is immortal—but it has nothing to do with "me." This "me" is not immortal, this "I" is not immortal. This "I" is just temporary; it is manufactured by us.

Fear is the shadow of "I." And because the "I" is always alert somewhere deep down it will have to disappear in death. . . . The basic fear is of death; all other fears only reflect the basic one. And the beauty is that death is as nonexistential as ego. So between these two nonexistentials, the ego and death, the bridge is fear.

Fear itself is impotent, it has no power. It is just that you want to believe in it—that's its only power. You are not ready to take a plunge into your inner depth and to face your inner emptiness—that is its power. Otherwise it is impotent, utterly impotent. Nothing is ever born out of fear. Love gives birth, love is creative; fear is impotent. It has never created anything. It cannot create anything because it has no substance. But it can destroy your whole life, it can surround you like a dark cloud, it can exploit all your energies. It will not allow you to move into any deep experience of beauty, poetry, love, joy, celebration, meditation. No, it will keep you just on the surface because it can exist only on the surface. It is a ripple on the surface.

Go in, look in . . . and if it is empty, so what? Then that's our nature, then that's what we are. Why should one be worried about emptiness? Emptiness is as beautiful as the sky. Your inner being is nothing but the inner sky. The sky is empty, but it is the empty sky that holds all, the whole existence, the sun, the moon, the stars, the earth, the planets. It is the empty sky that gives space to all that is. It is the empty sky that is the background of all that exists. Things come and go and the sky remains the same.

In exactly the same way, you have an inner sky; it is also empty. Clouds come and go, planets are born and disappear, stars arise and die, and the inner sky remains the same, untouched, untarnished, unscarred. We call that inner sky the witness, the watcher—and that is the whole goal of meditation.

Go in, enjoy the inner sky. Remember, whatsoever you can see, you are not it. You can see thoughts, then you are not thoughts; you can see your feelings, then you are not your feelings; you can see your dreams, desires, memories, imaginations, projections, then you are not those things. Go on eliminating all that you can see. Then one day the tremendous moment arrives, the most significant moment of one's life, when there is nothing left to be rejected. All the seen has disappeared and only the seer is there. That seer is the empty sky.

To know it is to be fearless, and to know it is to be full of love. To know it is to be god, is to be immortal.

Where Does Fear Come From? Where Does It Go?

Fear affects me in different ways, from a vague uneasiness or knotted stomach to a dizzying panic, as if the world is ending. Where does fear come from? Where does it go?

All your fears are by-products of identification.

You love a person and with the love, in the same parcel, comes fear—the person may leave you. They have already left somebody else and come with you, so there is a precedent; perhaps they will do the same to you. There is fear, you feel knots in the stomach. You are so attached, you cannot grasp a simple fact: You have come alone into the world. You have been here yesterday too, without this person, and you were doing perfectly well, without any knots in the stomach. Tomorrow, if this person goes . . . what is the need of the knots? You already know how to be without the person, and you will be able to be alone again.

The fear that things may change tomorrow . . . somebody may die, you may go bankrupt, your job may be taken away, there are a thousand and one things that might change. You are burdened with fears and fears, and none of them are valid—because yesterday also you were full of all these fears, unnecessarily. Things may have changed, but you are still alive. And people have an immense capacity to adjust themselves to any situation.

They say that only human beings and cockroaches have this immense capacity for adjustment. That's why wherever you find humans you will find cockroaches, and wherever you find cockroaches you will find human beings. They go together, they have a similarity. Even in faraway places like the North Pole or the South Pole—when people first traveled to those places they suddenly found they had brought cockroaches with them, and those roaches were perfectly healthy and living and reproducing.

If you just look around the earth you can see—man lives in thousands of different climates, geographical situations, political situations, sociological situations, religious situations, but he manages to live. And he has lived for centuries . . . things go on changing, he goes on adjusting himself.

There is nothing to fear. Even if the world ends, so what? You will be ending with it! Do you think you will be standing on an island and the whole world will end, leaving you alone? Don't be worried. At least you will have a few cockroaches with you!

What is the problem if the world ends? I have been asked about it many times, but what is the problem? If it ends, it ends. It does not create any problem because we will not be here; we will be ending with it, and there will be no one to worry about. It will be really the ultimate freedom from fear. The world ending means every problem ending, every disturbance ending, every knot in your stomach ending. I don't see the problem.

But I know that everybody is full of fear. Everybody has a kind of armor, and there are reasons for it. First, the child is born so utterly helpless, into a world he knows nothing of. Naturally he is afraid of the unknown that faces him. He has not yet forgotten those nine months of absolute security, safety, when there was no problem, no responsibility, no worry for tomorrow.

To us, those are nine months, but to the child it is eternity. He knows nothing of the calendar, he knows nothing of minutes, hours, days, months. He has lived an eternity in absolute safety and security, without any responsibility, and then suddenly he is thrown into a world unknown, where he is dependent for everything on others. It is natural that he will feel afraid. Everybody is bigger and more powerful, and he cannot live without the help of others. He knows he is dependent; he has lost his independence, his freedom.

A child is weak, vulnerable, insecure. Automatically he starts creating an armor, a protection for himself in different ways. For example, he has to sleep alone. It is dark and he is afraid, but he has his teddy bear and he convinces himself that he is not alone—his friend is with him. You will see children dragging their teddy bears at airports, at railway stations. Do you think it is just a toy? To you it is, but to the child it is a friend—and a friend when nobody else is there to help him—in the darkness of the night, alone in the bed, still the teddy bear is with him.

He will create psychological teddy bears. And remember that although a grown-up man may think that he has no teddy bears, he is wrong. What is his God? Just a teddy bear. Out of his childhood fear, man has created a father figure who knows all, who is all-powerful, who is everywhere present; if you have enough faith in him he will protect you. But the very idea of protection, the very idea that a protector is needed, is childish. Then you learn prayer—these are just parts of your psychological armor—prayer is to remind God that you are here, alone in the night.

Our prayers, chanting, mantras, our scriptures, our gods, our priests, are all part of our psychological armor. It is very subtle. A Christian believes that he will be saved and nobody else. Now, that is his defensive arrangement; everybody is going to fall into hell except him, because he is a Christian. But every religion believes, in the same way, that only they will be saved. It is not a question of the religion, it is a question of fear and being saved from fear. So it is natural in a way—but at a certain point in your maturity, intelligence demands that it should be dropped. It was good when you were a child, but one day you have to leave your teddy bear. Finally, the day you drop all your armor, it means you have dropped living out of fear. What kind of living can arise out of fear? Once the armor is dropped you can live out of love, you can live in a mature way. The fully matured person has no fear, no defense; he is psychologically open and vulnerable.

At one point, the armor may be a necessity—perhaps it is. But as you grow—if you are not only growing old but also growing up, growing in maturity—then you will start seeing what you are carrying with you. Look closely and you will find fear behind so many things.

A mature person should disconnect himself from anything that is connected with fear. That's how maturity comes.

Just watch all your acts, all your beliefs, and find out whether they are based in reality, in experience, or based in fear. Anything based in fear has to be dropped immediately, without a second thought. It is your armor.

I cannot melt it for you, I can simply show you how you can drop it. Your psychological armor cannot be taken away from you. You will fight for it. Only you can do something to drop it, and that is to look at each and every part of it. If it is based in fear, then drop it. If it is based in reason, in experience, in understanding, then it is not something to be dropped, it is something to be made part of your being. But you will not find a single thing in your armor that is based on experience. It is all fear, from A to Z.

We go on living out of fear—that's why we go on poisoning every other experience. We love somebody, but when our love comes out of fear it is spoiled, poisoned. We seek truth, but if the search is out of fear then you are not going to find it.

Whatever you do, remember one thing: Out of fear you are not going to grow. You will only shrink and die. Fear is in the service of death.

A fearless person has everything that life wants to give to you as a gift. Now there is no barrier. You will be showered with gifts, and whatever you do you will have a strength, a power, a certainty, a tremendous feeling of authority.

A person living out of fear is always trembling inside. He is continuously on the point of going insane, because life is big, and if you are continuously in fear . . . and fears of all kinds are available. You can make a big list, and you will be surprised how many fears are there—still you are alive! There are infections all around, diseases, dangers, kidnapping, terrorists . . . and such a small life! And finally there is death, which you cannot avoid. Your whole life will become dark.

Drop the fear—the fear was taken up by you in your childhood unconsciously; now consciously drop it and be mature. Then life can be a light that goes on deepening as you go on growing.

Buried Alive

I feel like I'm buried alive under my fear. And I see now that I've always been trying to be someone "special" to hide this fear, running further and further away from myself until I don't know anymore what it means to be real. Why do I feel such a need to hide behind masks? Why am I so afraid?

The fear you are suffering from is rooted in every being. It is bound to be so, because every day we know someone dies and we know that we are standing in the same queue. And whenever someone dies we are moving in the queue, closer to death. Soon we will be at the window to take a ticket to get out of existence.

The poet is right when he says, "Don't send anybody to ask for whom the bell tolls, it tolls for thee." When someone dies, there is an old tradition: In the churches the bells start tolling to inform the whole village, "Someone is dead—come back from your farms, your gardens, your orchards." It is a call to people that somebody has died and he has to be given the last send-off. But the poet is perfectly right, "Don't send anyone to ask for whom the bell tolls, it always tolls for thee." Whenever someone dies you are reminded again that you are a mortal being, that death can take possession of you at any moment.

This is the root fear; all other fears are reflections of it. If you go deep down into any fear, you will find the fear of death.

You are asking, "I feel like I am buried alive under my fear." Everybody is in the same situation. You are fortunate that you have become aware of it, because if you are aware, you can come out. And if you are unaware then there is no possibility of coming out.

You say, "I have always been trying to be someone special to hide this fear, running further and further away from myself until I don't know anymore what it means to be real."

Do you think the people who are special are doing something else? The presidents and the prime ministers and the kings and the queens—do you think they are in a different boat? Just look around and you will find them all in the same boat. They are all trying to be special in the hope that perhaps if they are special, life will treat them differently than it treats ordinary people. Obviously it cannot treat a president of a country the same way it treats a shoemaker.

But they are absolutely wrong. Life makes no discriminations—presidents or shoemakers, toilet cleaners or prime ministers, it does not matter at all as far as life is concerned. Death knocks them off with equality. Death is the only communist in the world; it does not care whether you have money or you are a beggar, you are educated or uneducated. You cannot say, "Just wait, I am highly qualified. You cannot behave the way you behave with uneducated people. Just wait a little . . . I am a special person, you cannot behave this way. First, give me a little advance notice and I will consider it. You have to follow a certain procedure that will be decided by me." Whether you are a respected member of the community or just a stray dog, it makes no difference—death comes and makes everybody equal.

But the hope is that if you are special, existence will treat you with some kindness, some compassion. It will think twice, "The man is a Nobel Prize winner, you should just give him a little more life. The poor fellow is a great painter, you should not blow out his candle just the way you do with everybody else."

This is the hidden desire, unconscious hope, the reason why everybody goes on trying to be special. But it is absolutely foolish and absurd. Just look back at what has happened to the millions of kings and millions of queens who were so powerful. . . .

Before death everybody is absolutely powerless.

In Jaina scriptures there is a very beautiful story. In India there is a myth that if a man becomes a world conqueror he has a special name—he is no ordinary king, not even an emperor. He is called a *chakravartin*. It means that the wheel of his chariot can move around the earth anywhere, nobody can hinder it. He is all-powerful, and the myth says that in heaven the *chakravartins* are treated in a special way.

There is a golden mountain in heaven . . . the Himalayas is nothing but a very small toy in comparison to the gold mountain in heaven called Sumeru. Only *chakravartins* have the special privilege of signing their name on Sumeru. And when this *chakravartin* died, he was so excited . . . to sign one's name on the gold mountain in heaven is the greatest privilege that any human being can ever attain.

But what is the use if you are alone there to see it? So this man decreed that his whole court—his queen, his friends, his generals—should all commit suicide immediately, the moment he dies, so that they all reach heaven simultaneously. He wanted to sign on the gold mountain as nobody else had ever done it before. Signing alone, without even a witness—what is the joy in it? He must have been a perfect exhibitionist.

Because of his orders, all his friends, his queens, the members of his court, his generals, all committed suicide as he died and they all entered the gates of heaven together. The gatekeeper stopped them and he said, "Let the *chakravartin* go alone first to sign on the mountain."

But they said, "We have committed suicide only for a simple purpose: We want our *chakravartin* to sign before all of us. His queens are here, his generals are here, his wise counselors are here, his ministers are here . . . and we have even sacrificed our lives just to see him sign. You cannot prevent us."

But the gatekeeper said to the *chakravartin*, "Forgive me, I have

been on this post for centuries and before that my father, and before that my grandfather; this post has been occupied by my forefathers since the very beginning of time. And I have been told by my
elders, 'Never allow any *chakravartin* to go to the mountain in front
of others because he will repent it very badly later on.' But the
chakravartins all insist. . . . You are not the first who has brought a
whole army with him; almost every *chakravartin* has done the same.

"So I simply want you to remember that you will repent if I
allow these people to go with you. I have no problem, you can
have some time to think it over. You are new, you don't know
what the experience is going to be. I have seen many *chakravartins*
coming and going and they have all thanked me afterward and
said, 'You are very kind that you prevented everybody else and
sent me alone.'"

The *chakravartin* thought, "What to do? Because I do not
know what is actually going to happen, and this man seems to be
authentic and sincere and he has no reason to prevent me unnecessarily. . . . Perhaps it is better to listen to his advice." So he
stopped everybody at the gate, he took the instruments from the
gatekeeper to go and sign on the gold, and he went inside the gate
to the mountain. He could not believe . . . such beauty! As far as
he could see there was all gold and gold—mountain peaks reaching so high that the Himalayas certainly looked like a toy.

As he came closer to find a place to sign, he was shocked because there was no space! The whole mountain was signed . . .
because we have been here for eternity. Millions and millions of
chakravartins have died. This man had been thinking, "I am very
special"—and there was not even a little space left on this big
mountain!

He moved around—no space anywhere. Then he came across the caretaker of the mountain, who said, "Don't waste your time. Even if you search for a millennium, you will not find any empty space; all the space is filled. For centuries I have been serving here. My father has served here—from the very beginning my family has been at this job. And I have heard from my forefathers the same story, that whenever any *chakravartin* has come, there was no space. So the only way is to erase one of the other names and sign your name in its place, and forget all about being special. It is such a vast existence. That's why the gatekeeper prevented the people you brought; before all those people you would have lost all pride. You can just erase another name; I will help, I am here."

The whole joy was gone, the whole excitement was gone, and the *chakravartin* said to the man, "It just means somebody else will come tomorrow and he will erase my name." The mountain caretaker said, "That, of course, is the case—because there is no space otherwise. We cannot create more mountain; all the gold in heaven has been used to create this one. You simply sign, and back at the gate you can go with your head high and you can brag about it. Nobody is going to know because I am not going to tell anybody. Just go and brag that the whole mountain was empty."

But the *chakravartin* was a man of some integrity and truth. He said, "That I cannot do; neither can I erase any name to make room for mine. I am not going to sign—it is absolutely stupid." He went back and he told the gatekeeper, "I am thankful to you and I am going to tell my people why I am thankful. I am going to spread the news in the world, because many of these people have committed suicide. They will have to be born again, they cannot remain in heaven.

"I will make every effort to send the message to the world: 'Don't unnecessarily waste your life in conquering the world to sign on the gold mountain in heaven. There is no space. First you have to erase somebody else's name, which is ugly, and then you have to sign in that place and tomorrow somebody else will erase your name. The whole exercise is one of utter stupidity.' I am shocked, but a great realization has arisen in me: One should not ask to be special, because existence does not accept anybody as special, superior or inferior."

Your fear is driving you toward trying to be special but that will not change the situation. The only way the fear can be dropped is, rather than putting your energy into being special, put your whole energy into being yourself. Just find yourself, because in trying to be special you are running further and further away from yourself. That you are clearly aware of it is good: the further away you go from yourself, the further away you are from knowing the truth that you are an immortal, that there is no death.

Once you recognize your immortality, death disappears. And with death, all fears evaporate into the air. But not by becoming someone special.

You will go on running further and further away from yourself in search of something that can take away your fear, your paranoia, your death. But the further away you are the more will be the fear, the more will be the paranoia, the more overwhelming will be the death. It is better to go inward and find your real being.

This is a simple logic, a simple arithmetic: Before searching anywhere else, please search within yourself. The world is vast, you will be lost in the search . . . so first look within yourself; maybe what you are looking for is already there. And all the great enlightened people of the world are absolutely in agreement that it is there, without any exception.

This is the only scientific truth that has no exception—which has remained unchanged as far back as you can go. You will find it has always been declared by those who have known themselves, "We are immortal; we are deathless. Life knows no end."

So first, go in. Just a glimpse of your own immortality, and it is as if one has awakened from a nightmare. All the fear disappears, and instead of fear there is nothing but pure bliss, pure joy—just flowers showering with the fragrance of eternity.

So Much to Do, So Little Time

I have become aware that I have a lot of anxiety about time. I've heard you say that time consciousness creates frustration, but I wonder—is there something within us that could be called a fear of time?

That is the only fear there is: the fear of time. The fear of death is also fear of time because death stops all time. Nobody is afraid of death—how can you be afraid of something that you have not known? How can you be afraid of the absolutely unknown, unfamiliar, strange? Fear can only exist with something which is known. No, when you say, "I am afraid of death" you are not afraid of death—you don't know! Who knows?—death may be better than life.

The fear is not of death, the fear is of time.

In India we have the same term for both. Time we call *kala* and death also we call *kala*. We have one term for both death and time. It is meaningful, the word *kala* is meaningful, very significant, because time is death, and death is nothing but time.

Time passing means life passing. Fear arises. In the West the fear is more acute; it has almost become chronic. In the East the fear is not so much, and the reason is that the East believes that life continues forever and ever; death is not the end; this life is not the only life; there have been thousands and thousands of lives in the past and there will be thousands and thousands in the future. There is no hurry. That's why the East is lazy: There is no hurry! That's why in the East there is no time-consciousness—somebody says, "I will come at five o'clock sharp, and he never turns up." He does not feel any responsibility toward time, and you are waiting and waiting, and he comes four, five hours late and he says, "What is wrong in it? So what?"

In the Western perspective time is very short, because Christianity and Judaism both believe in only one life. That has created the anxiety. There is only one life, seventy years at the most; one-third lost in sleep—if you live sixty years, twenty years are lost in sleep, twenty of the remaining years are lost in education, this and that; the remaining twenty years—the job, the occupation, the family, marriage and divorce, and if you really calculate you will find there is no time to live! "When will I live?" Fear grips the heart, and life is passing, time is flowing out of your hands and death is reaching every moment with such a constant pace—any moment it can knock at the door. And time is irrecoverable, you cannot get it back, gone—gone forever.

Fear, anxiety, a time neurosis—it is becoming chronic, it is almost as if it has become second nature to the Western mind, continuously alert that time is slipping away, and afraid.

The fear is basically that you have not yet been able to live, and time is passing, and it cannot be recovered, you cannot undo it; gone—gone forever. And every day life is shrinking, becoming smaller and smaller and smaller.

The fear is not of death, the fear is of time, and if you look deeply into it then you find that the fear is of unlived life—you have not been able to live. If you live, then there is no fear. If life comes to a fulfillment, there is no fear. If you have enjoyed, attained to the peaks that life can give, if your life has been an orgasmic experience, a deep poetry vibrating within you, a song, a festival, a ceremony, and you lived each moment of it to its totality, then there is no fear of time, then the fear disappears.

You are ready even if death comes today, you are ready. You have known life—in fact you will welcome death because now a new opportunity opens, a new door, a new mystery is revealed: I have lived life, now death is knocking at the door; I will jump to open the door—"Come in!" Because life I have known, I would like to know you also.

That's what happened to Socrates when he was dying. His disciples started crying and weeping—and it was natural. Socrates opened his eyes and said, "Stop! What are you doing? Why are you crying and weeping? I have lived my life, and I have lived it totally. Now death is coming and I'm enthusiastic about it! I am waiting with such great love and longing, with hope. A new door opens, life reveals a new mystery."

Somebody asked, "Are you not afraid?"

Socrates said, "I don't see the point in being afraid of death, because in the first place I don't know what is going to be. And secondly, there are only two possibilities: Either I will survive—

then there is no question of fear. Or I will not survive—then too there is no problem of fear. If I don't survive there is no problem—when I am not, there cannot be any problem, and if I survive as I am here, if my consciousness survives, there is no problem because I am still there.

"Problems were there in life also—I solved them, so if I am there and there are problems I will solve them—and it is always a joy to solve a problem, it gives a challenge. You take the challenge and you move into it, and when you solve it a great release of happiness happens."

The fear of death is fear of time, and the fear of time is, deeply, the fear of unlived moments, an unlived life.

So what to do? Live more, and live more intensely. Live dangerously! It is your life, don't sacrifice it for any sort of foolishness that has been taught to you. It is your life, live it. Don't sacrifice it for words, theories, countries, politics. Don't sacrifice it for anybody.

There are many who are ready like butchers; they can get hold of you. And they have implanted conditionings within you: "Your nation is in danger—die for it!" Absolute foolishness. "Your religion is in danger—die for it!" Nonsense—it is your life, live it! Don't die for anything else, die only for life, that's the message. And then there will be no fear. But there are people who are ready to exploit you. They go on saying, "Die for this, die for that." They are ready for only one thing, that you should become a martyr. Then there will be fears.

Live life, and don't think that it is a courageous thing to die. The only courage is to live life totally, there is no other courage. Dying is very simple and easy. You can go and jump off a cliff, you can hang yourself—it is such an easy thing. You can become a martyr to a country, to a god, to a religion, to a church—all butchers, all murderers. Don't sacrifice yourself. You are here for yourself, for nobody else.

And then live. And live in total freedom so intensely that every moment is transformed into eternity. If you live a moment intensely it is transformed into eternity. If you live a moment intensely you move into the vertical, you drop out of the horizontal.

There are two ways of being related with time: One is just to swim on the surface of the ocean, another is to dive deep, to go to the depths.

If you are just swimming on the ocean of time you will be always afraid because the surface is not the reality. The surface is not really the ocean, it is just the boundary, it is just the periphery. Go to the depth, move toward the depth. When you live a moment deeply you are no more part of time.

If you have been in love, and deeply in love, time disappears. When you are with your beloved or your lover or your friend suddenly there is no time. You are moving in depth. If you have loved music, if you have a musical heart, you know time stops. If you have the sense of beauty, aesthetic sensibility and sensitiveness—look at a rose and time disappears, look at the moon and where is time? The clock immediately stops. The hands go on moving but time stops.

If you have loved anything deeply you know that you transcend time. The secret has been revealed to you many times. Life itself reveals it to you.

Life would like you to enjoy. Life would like you to celebrate. Life would like you to participate so deeply that there is no repentance for the past, that you don't remember the past, because every moment you go more and more deep—every moment life becomes more and more beautiful, more orgasmic, a peak experience, and by and by, when you become attuned to the peak, that becomes your abode.

That's how an enlightened man lives, he lives totally and moment to moment.

Somebody asked a Zen Master: Since enlightenment what have you been doing? He said: I carry water from the well, I cut wood in the forest, when I feel hungry I eat, and when I feel sleepy I sleep, that's all.

But remember well, when a man who has come to a deep understanding of his own being cuts wood, he simply cuts wood. There is nobody else there. In fact the cutter is not there, only the cutting of the wood, the chopping. The chopper is not there because the chopper is the past. When he eats he simply eats.

One great Zen Master has said: When sitting sit, when walking walk, above all, don't wobble.

Time is a problem because you have not been living rightly—it is symbolic, it is symptomatic. If you live rightly the problem of time disappears, the fear of time disappears.

So, what to do? Each moment, whatsoever you are doing, do it totally. Simple things—taking a bath; take it totally, forget the whole world; sitting, sit; walking, walk, above all don't wobble; sit under the shower and let the whole existence fall on you. Be merged with those beautiful drops of water falling on you. Small things: cleaning the house, preparing food, washing clothes, going for a morning walk—do them totally, then there is no need for any meditation.

Meditation is nothing but a way to learn how to do a thing totally—once you have learned, make your whole life a meditation; forget all about meditations, let the life be the only law, let the life be the only meditation. And then time disappears.

And remember, when time disappears, death disappears. Then you are not afraid of death. In fact you wait.

Just think of the phenomenon. When you wait for death how can death exist?

This waiting is not suicidal. This waiting is not pathological. You lived your life. If you have lived your life, death becomes the very peak of it all. Death is the climax of life, the pinnacle, the crescendo.

You lived all small waves of eating, drinking, sleeping, walking, making love, small waves, great waves, you lived—then comes the greatest wave. You die! You have to live that too in its totality. And then one is ready to die. That very readiness is the death of death itself.

That's how people have come to know that nothing dies. Death is impotent if you are ready to live it, death is very powerful if you are afraid. Unlived life gives power to death. A totally lived life takes all power from death. Death is not.

Understanding Is the Key

How can fear be mastered, or eliminated altogether?

Fear cannot be eliminated altogether, it cannot be mastered, it can only be understood. Understanding is the key word here. And only understanding brings mutation, nothing else. If you try to master your fear it will remain repressed, it will go deep into you. It will not help, it will complicate things. It is surfacing, you can repress it—that's what mastery is. You can repress it; you can repress it so deeply that it disappears from your consciousness completely. Then you will never be aware of it, but it will be there in the basement, and it will have a pull. It will manage, it will manipulate you, but it will manipulate you in such an indirect way that you will not become aware of it. But then the danger has gone deeper. Now you cannot even understand it.

So fear has not to be mastered—it has not to be eliminated. It cannot be eliminated either, because fear contains a kind of energy and no energy can be destroyed. Have you seen that in fear you can have immense energy? Just as you can have in anger; they are both two aspects of the same energy phenomenon. Anger is aggressive and fear is nonaggressive. Fear is anger in a negative state; anger is fear in a positive state. When you are angry have you not watched how powerful you become, how great an energy you have? You can throw a big rock when you are angry; ordinarily you cannot even shake it. You become thrice, four times bigger when you are angry. You can do certain things you cannot do without anger.

Or, in fear, you can run so fast that even an Olympic runner will feel jealous. Fear creates energy; fear *is* energy, and energy cannot be destroyed. Not a single iota of energy can be eliminated from existence. This has to be remembered constantly, otherwise you will do something wrong. You cannot destroy anything, you can only change its form. You cannot destroy a small pebble; a small grain of sand cannot be destroyed, it will only change its form. You cannot destroy a drop of water. You can turn it into ice, you can evaporate it, but it will remain. It will remain somewhere, it cannot go out of existence.

You cannot destroy fear either. And that has been tried down the ages—people have been trying to destroy fear, trying to destroy anger, trying to destroy sexuality, trying to destroy greed, this and that. The whole world has been continuously working to destroy your energies, and what is the result? Man has become a mess. Nothing is destroyed, all is still there; only things have become confused. There is no need to try to destroy anything because nothing can be destroyed in the first place.

Then what has to be done? You have to understand fear. What is fear? How does it arise? From where does it come? What is its message? Look into it—and without any judgment; only then will you understand. If you already have an idea that fear is wrong, that it should not exist—"I should not be afraid"—then you cannot look. How can you confront fear? How can you look into the eyes of fear when you have already decided that it is your enemy? Nobody looks into the eyes of the enemy. If you think it is something wrong, then you will try to bypass it, avoid it, neglect it. You will try not to come across it, but it will remain. This is not going to help.

First drop all condemnation, judgment, evaluation. Fear is a reality. It has to be faced, it has to be understood. And only through understanding can it be transformed. In fact, it is transformed through understanding. There is no need to do anything else; understanding transforms it.

What is fear? First, fear is always around some desire. You want to become a famous man, the most famous man in the world—then there is fear. What if you cannot make it? Fear comes. Now fear comes as a by-product of desire. You want to become the richest man in the world. What if you don't succeed? You start trembling; fear comes. You want to possess a woman and you are afraid that tomorrow you may not be able to hold on to her, she may go to somebody else. She is still alive, she can go. Only a dead woman won't be able to go, and this woman is still alive. You can possess a corpse—then there is no fear, the corpse will be there. You can possess furniture, then there is no fear. But when you try to possess a human being fear comes. Who knows, yesterday she was not yours, today she is yours . . . who knows? Tomorrow she might be somebody else's. Fear arises. Fear is arising out of the desire to possess, it is a by-product; you want to possess, hence the fear. If you don't want to possess, then there is no fear. If you don't have a desire that you would like to be this and that in the future, then there is no fear. If you don't want to go to heaven then there is no fear, then the priest cannot make you afraid. If you don't want to go anywhere then nobody can make you afraid.

If you start living in the moment, fear disappears. Fear comes through desire. So basically, desire creates fear.

Look into it. Whenever there is fear, see from where it is coming, what desire is creating it, and then see the futility of it. How can you possess a woman or a man? It is such a silly, stupid idea! Only things can be possessed, not persons.

A person is a freedom. A person is beautiful because of freedom. The bird is beautiful on the wing in the sky—you encage it and it is no longer the same bird, remember. It looks like it, but it is no longer the same bird. Where is the sky? Where is the sun, where are those winds, where are those clouds? Where is that freedom on the wing? All have disappeared. This is not the same bird.

You love a woman because she is a freedom. Then you encage her: Then you go to the court and you get married, and you make

a beautiful cage around her, maybe golden, studded with diamonds, but she is no longer the same woman. And now fear comes.
You are afraid, afraid because the woman may not like this cage.
She may hanker for freedom again. And freedom is an ultimate
value, one cannot drop it.

Man consists of freedom, consciousness consists of freedom. So
sooner or later the woman will start feeling bored, fed up. She will
start looking for somebody else. You are afraid. Your fear is coming because you want to possess—but why in the first place do you
want to possess? Be nonpossessive, and then there is no fear. And
when there is no fear, much of the energy that gets involved and
caught up, locked up in fear, is available—and that energy can
become your creativity. It can become a dance, a celebration.

You are afraid to die? You cannot die, because in the first
place, you are not. How can you die? Look into your being, go
deep into it. Who is there to die? When you look deeply, you will
not find any ego, any "self" there. Then there is no possibility of
death. Only the idea of ego creates the fear of death. When there
is no ego there is no death. You are utter silence, deathlessness,
eternity—not as you, but as an open sky, uncontaminated by any
idea of "I," of self—unbounded, undefined. Then there is no fear.

Fear comes because there are other things. You will have to
look into those things, and looking into them will start changing
things.

So please don't ask how it can be mastered or destroyed. It is
not to be mastered, it is not to be eliminated. It cannot be mastered and it cannot be destroyed, it can only be understood. Let
understanding be your only law.

Divine Insecurity

*I know that any idea of external security is foolish and unrealistic,
but isn't there an internal security that we can strive for?*

There is no security, internal or external. Security exists not,
that's why existence is so beautiful. Just think of a rose flower in
the morning that starts thinking about being secure; then what
will happen? If the rose flower really becomes secure it will become a plastic flower; otherwise insecurity is there. A strong
wind may come and the petals will be gone. A child will come
running and will pick the flower. A goat will come rushing and
eat it. Or nothing may happen—no child comes and no goat and
no wind, but by the evening it will be gone. Even if nothing out
of the ordinary happens, then too it will be gone.

But that is the beauty of the rose flower, that's why it is so
beautiful—because it lives surrounded by death, it challenges
death, it challenges the winds. Such a small, tiny flower, and such
a great challenge, and it rises above all difficulties and dangers.
Even if it is only for a few minutes or a few hours—that doesn't
matter, time is immaterial—it has its own day. It has lived, it has
talked with the winds and talked with the sun and the moon and
looked at the clouds. And there was joy, there was great passion!
Then it dies; it doesn't cling. A clinging rose flower will be ugly;
only human beings become that ugly. When the time comes the
flower simply dies and disappears into the earth from where it
came. There is no external security, no internal security. Insecurity is the very stuff that life is made of.

That is the difference between my work and other people's

work—they give you security, I take away all security from you. I make you aware of the beauties of life—its risks, dangers, its insecurities. I make you more sensitive. And in that greater sensitivity there is great challenge and adventure. Then one does not bother whether tomorrow is going to happen or not; today is more than enough. If we can love, if we can live, this day is more than enough.

A single moment of deep love is eternity. Who bothers about security? The very idea arises out of greed, the very idea arises out of ego. Call it internal security, call it external security, it won't make any difference. One has to look through and through and one has to see that there is no security and that it is not possible in the very situation of existence. In that very moment a great revolution has moved into your being; you are metamorphosed.

Jesus calls that moment *metanoia*. You are converted . . . not that you become a Christian or you become a Catholic or a Protestant. In that moment you are no longer worldly.

To search for security is to be worldly. To live in insecurity like a rose flower is to be otherworldly.

Security is of the world; insecurity is of the divine.

2

SCARED TO DEATH—
EXPLORING
THE ROOTS OF FEAR

When people are living in fear, their lives are not very alive. Fear cripples and paralyzes. It cuts your roots, it does not allow you to attain to your full height, to your full being. It keeps people pygmies, spiritual pygmies. To grow to your destiny needs great courage, it needs fearlessness, and fearlessness is the most religious quality.

People who are full of fear cannot move beyond the known. The known gives a kind of comfort, security, safety because it is known. One is perfectly aware. One knows how to deal with it. One can remain almost asleep and go on dealing with it—there is no need to be awake; that's the convenience with the known.

The moment you cross the boundary of the known, fear arises because now you will be ignorant, now you will not know what to do, what not to do. Now you will not be so sure of yourself, now mistakes can be committed; you can go astray. That is the fear that keeps people tethered to the known, and once a person is tethered to the known he is dead.

Life can only be lived dangerously—there is no other way to live it. It is only through danger that life attains to maturity, growth. One needs to be an adventurer, always ready to risk the known for the unknown. And once one has tasted the joys of freedom and fearlessness, one never repents because then one knows what it means to live at the optimum. Then one knows what it means to burn your life's torch from both ends together. And even a single moment of that intensity is more gratifying than the whole eternity of mediocre living.

One is afraid of death because one is unaware of what life is. If you know what life is, the fear of death disappears of its own accord. The question is not of death at all, the question is of life. Because we don't know what life is, hence we are afraid that it is going to end one day. We have not even lived. How can you live without knowing what it is? You have neither lived nor loved; you have simply been dragging, vegetating. And you know that one thing is certain: Death is coming closer every day, every moment; hence the fear. The fear is natural because death will close the door forever. Without ever knowing what life was, you will be taken away. You were given an opportunity, a great opportunity, and you missed it.

You go on postponing for tomorrow. You say, "Tomorrow I am going to live." But simultaneously, side-by-side, you know there is a fear: "Tomorrow, who knows? Tomorrow maybe death will come, then what?" You have postponed life for tomorrow and there is no more tomorrow—then what? Then fear arises.

And you don't know how to live right now. Nobody tells you how to live right now. The preachers, the politicians, the parents, they all tell you about the tomorrows. When you are a child they tell you, "When you are a young man then you will know what life is." When you are a young man they say, "You are young fools—youth is foolishness. When you are old, then you will understand." And when you are old they say, "You are finished. Now there is nothing left, you are like a used cartridge." This is a strange world!

In my childhood, as it happens in every child's life, I used to ask all the elders available thousands of questions. It almost became a torture for them because my questions were embarrassing to them. So the easiest way for them was to say, "You are too young. Wait."

One of my father's friends was known in the whole town as a sage. I used to go with my father to see him and I used to torture him the most. He would always say, "Wait. You are too young and your questions are too complicated. When you are a little more grown-up, then you will be able to understand."

I asked him, "You please give me in writing what year I will be grown up. Then I will ask you these questions. Because this is tricky of you! Whenever I ask—and I have been asking for at least five years—you always say the same thing: 'When you grow up . . .' You might keep on saying this to me again and again forever! So just write the year down on paper and sign it."

I saw his hand was shaking. I said, "Why is your hand shaking?

Why are you afraid? If you know at what age a person becomes able to understand, write it on the paper. If you say at age twenty, I will ask at twenty-one—I will give you one year more!"

So he wrote, "Twenty-one years."

So I said, "Okay, I will come back only when I am twenty-two."

He must have thought, "At least the problem is solved for the time being. Who knows? After he is twenty-two . . . ?" I must have been at that time near about fourteen.

Exactly when I became twenty-two I went back, and I arrived with a crowd—I had gathered many people to come with me, and I said to him, "This is your letter. Now answer!"

He said, "You are such a nuisance! Why have you brought all these people?"

I said, "Just to witness that you have been cheating me. And not only have you been cheating me, this has been going on all over the world. Every elderly person is cheating young people, telling them, 'tomorrow,' and the tomorrow never comes. Now I am twenty-two years old and you have written 'Twenty-one years' on the paper. I have given you one year more just in case I am not intelligent enough and have taken a little longer to grow up. But now I am not going to leave, I will stay here until all my questions are answered."

He said, "To tell you the truth, I don't know anything. And please don't ask me again. Forgive me, you are right—I have been lying to you."

"Why did you lie to a child?" I asked him. "How could you lie to a child who was asking out of such innocence, who trusted you? And you deceived him! You don't know whether God exists or not, but you were telling me that God exists and that I would be able to understand later on. I knew that very moment that you didn't understand. You don't know anything about God, you are just repeating like a parrot."

But this is the situation; teachers don't know, professors don't know, priests don't know, but without knowing they go on pretending they know. And the whole strategy consists of a single trick, and that is to go on postponing: "You will also know when the time is ripe." Of course it is never ripe, you never grow up. And by the time you are old enough you have to save your own face, so you start saying the same things to your children.

If you love your children, if you love your younger brothers, sisters, never tell lies to them. Be truthful, tell them, "I don't know and I am searching." Don't postpone it for tomorrow.

Our whole life is a postponement, hence the fear of death: "I have not known yet, and death is coming." Everybody is afraid of death for the simple reason that we have not tasted of life yet. The man who knows what life is, is never afraid of death; he welcomes death. Whenever death comes he embraces it, he welcomes it, he receives death as a guest. To the man who has not known what life is, death is an enemy. And to the man who knows what life is, death is the ultimate crescendo of life.

But everybody is afraid of death; that too is contagious. Your parents are afraid of death, your neighbors are afraid of death. Small children start getting infected by this constant fear all around. Everybody is afraid of death. People don't even want to talk about it.

When a man dies, there are experts to decorate the body. The person may never have looked so beautiful as he looks after death—painted, and his cheeks so rosy as if he had just come from a three-month vacation in Florida! Looking so healthy, as if he had just been exercising, and now he is doing the death posture in yoga, he is not really dead. The impression has to be created that he is not dead. Even on the gravestone it is written, "He is not dead, he is only asleep." And in all the languages, whenever somebody dies, nobody says that he is simply dead. We say, "He has gone to heaven. He has become a beloved of God; God has chosen him and called him. He has gone to the other world." You talk about people's divinity only when they are dead.

Once a man dies, nobody speaks against him, nobody says anything against him. He becomes suddenly a saint, suddenly great. His place will never be filled again, the world will always miss him, he was so essential. And nobody had taken any notice while he was alive! These are tricks—tricks to keep death away, to shut the doors and to forget all about death.

A real humanity will not have any taboos—no taboo about sex, no taboo about death. Life should be lived in its totality, and death is part of life. One should live totally and one should die totally.

When I work with people in depth in therapy, three fears continually come up in them. It's the fear of going crazy, it's the fear of letting go in sexual orgasm, and the fear of dying. These three fears come up over and over again in my work. Can you please comment on this?

It is really very significant, an existential question.

Humanity has lived in these three fears for thousands of years. They are not personal, they are collective. They come from the collective unconscious.

The fear of going crazy is in everyone, for the simple reason that their intelligence has not been allowed to develop. Intelligence is dangerous to the vested interests, so for thousands of years they have been cutting its very roots.

In Japan they have a certain type of tree that is thought to be a great art, but it is simply murder. The trees are four hundred, five hundred years old and six inches high. Generations of gardeners have taken care of them. The technique is that the trees are put in a pot without any bottom, and they go on cutting the roots. They don't allow the roots of the trees to go into the earth. And when you don't allow the roots to go deeper, the tree simply grows old, it never grows up. It is a strange phenomenon to see that type of tree. It looks ancient, but it has only grown old, older and older; it has never grown up. It has never blossomed, it has never given any fruits.

That is exactly the situation of man. His roots are cut; man lives almost uprooted. He has to be made uprooted so that he can become dependent on the society, on the culture, on the religion, on the state, on the parents, on everybody. He has to depend, he himself has no roots. The moment he becomes aware that he has no roots he feels he is going crazy, he is going insane. He is losing every support, he is falling into a dark ditch . . . because his knowledge is borrowed, it is not his own. His respectability is borrowed. He himself has no respect for his own being. His whole personality is borrowed from some source—the university, the church, the state. He himself has nothing of his own.

Just think of a man who lives in a grand palace with every conceivable luxury, and one day suddenly you make him aware that the palace does not belong to him, and neither do these luxuries belong to him. You tell him, "They belong to somebody else who is coming and you will be thrown out." He will go crazy. So in deep therapy you will come across this point, and the person has to face it and allow it, to go crazy.

Allow the situation in the therapy that the person can go crazy—once he goes crazy, he will drop the fear. Now he knows what craziness is. The fear is always of the unknown. Let him go crazy and he will soon calm down, because there is no real base to his fear. It is a fear projected by the society.

The parents say, "If you don't follow us, if you disobey, you will be condemned." The Jewish God says in Talmud, "I am a very jealous God, very angry God. Remember that I am not nice, I am not your uncle." All the religions have been doing it, and if you just leave the way that is followed by the mob they will declare you crazy. So everybody goes on clinging to the crowd, remaining part of a religion, a church, a party, a nation, a race. The person is afraid to be alone, and that's what you are doing when you bring him to his own depths. All that crowd, all those connections disappear. He's left alone and there is nobody else on whom he has always depended.

He has nothing of his own intelligence—that is the problem. Unless he starts growing his own intelligence, he will always remain afraid of being crazy. Not only that, the society can make him crazy any moment. If the society wants to make him crazy, if that is in their favor, they will make him crazy.

In the Soviet Union it used to happen almost every day. I am taking the example of the Soviet Union because they did it more scientifically, methodologically. It happens everywhere all over the world, but their methods are very primitive. For example, in India if a person behaves in a way that is not approved, he is made an outcast. He cannot get any support from anyone in the town. People will not even speak to him. His own family will close the doors in his face. The man is bound to go crazy, you are driving him crazy!

But in Soviet Russia they did it more methodologically and they have done it to such people who were Nobel Prize winners, who had intelligence—but an intelligence that was always under control, under the supervision of the state. And just a single act of disobedience . . . because the person got the Nobel Prize and the Soviet government did not want them to have it, because that prize came from a capitalist world, and to the government it seemed like bribery. This was how they purchased people, and these were the people who had all the secrets of science. They didn't want them to be world-known, they didn't want them to be in contact with other scientists; they wouldn't allow them to accept the Nobel Prize. But if the person insisted, then the result was that he was put into a hospital.

He goes on saying, "I am perfectly healthy; why am I being put in the hospital?" They say, "Because the doctors feel you are going to be sick. The early symptoms are there, you may not be aware." And they go on injecting the person, he knows nothing of what they are doing, and within fifteen days he is mad. They have made him mad through their chemicals. And when he is perfectly mad, then they produce him in the court, saying that "this man is insane, and he should be removed from his job and should be sent into a mental asylum." And then nobody ever hears what happened to those people. This is doing it scientifically. But every society has been doing it, and the fear has entered into very deep realms of the unconscious.

The work of therapy is to make the person free of that fear. If he is free of that fear, he is free of society, free of culture, free of religion, free of God, heaven, hell, and all nonsense. All that nonsense is significant because of this fear, and to make that non-sense significant the fear has been created.

It is the ugliest crime one can think of. It is being done to every child around the world every moment, and the people who are do-ing it have no bad intentions. They think they are doing something for the good of the child. They have been conditioned by their parents, and they are transferring the same conditioning to their children. But basically the whole humanity stands on the verge of madness. In deep therapy the fear grips the person suddenly, be-cause he is losing all the props, supports; the crowd is disappearing farther and farther away; he is being left alone. Suddenly there is darkness and there is fear. He has never been trained, disciplined for being alone. And that is the function of meditation. No ther-apy is complete without meditation, because only meditation can give him his lost roots, his strength of being an individual. There is nothing to fear. But the conditioning is that you have to be afraid of each moment, each step.

The whole humanity lives in paranoia. This humanity could have lived in paradise; it is living in hell. So help the person to understand that this is nothing to be worried about, there is noth-ing to be afraid of. It is a created fear. Every child is born fearless. He can play with snakes with no fear, the child has no idea of fear or death or anything. Meditation brings the person back to his childhood. He is reborn.

So help the person to understand why the fear exists. Make it clear that it is a phony phenomenon, imposed upon him: "So there is no need to be worried: In this situation you can go crazy. Don't be afraid. Enjoy that for the first time you have a situation in which you can be crazy and yet not condemned but loved, respected." And the group has to respect the person, love the person—he needs it, and he will cool down. And he will come out of the fear with a great freedom, with great stamina, strength, integrity.

The second fear is of sexual orgasm. That too is created by religions. All religions exist because they have turned man against his own energies. Sex is man's whole energy, his life energy, and religious prophets and messiahs, messengers of God, they all are doing the same work—in different words, different languages, but their work is the same, to make man an enemy of himself. And the basic strategy—because sex is the most powerful energy in you—is that sex should be condemned, guilt should be created. Then a problem arises for the individual. His nature is sensuous, sexual, and his mind is full of garbage against it. He is in a split. Neither can he drop his nature, nor can he drop the mind, because dropping the mind means dropping the society, the religion, the prophet, Jesus Christ, and God, everything. He's not capable to do that unless he has become an individual and is able to be alone without any fear.

So man is afraid of sex as far as his mind is concerned, but his biology has nothing to do with the mind. The biology has not received any information from the mind, there is no communication. The biology has its own way of functioning, so the biology will draw him toward sex and his mind will be standing there continuously condemning him. So he makes love, but in a hurry. That hurry has a very psychological reason. The hurry is that he is doing something wrong. He is doing something against God, against religion. He is feeling guilty and he cannot manage not to do it, so the only compromise is to do it, but be quick! That avoids the orgasm.

Now there are implications upon implications. A man who has not known orgasm feels unfulfilled, frustrated, angry, because he has never been in a state which nature provides freely, where he could have relaxed totally and become one with existence, at least for few moments. Because of his hurry he cannot manage the orgasm. Sex has become equivalent to ejaculation. That is not true as far as nature is concerned. Ejaculation is only a part, which you can manage without orgasm. You can reproduce children, so biology is not worried about your orgasm. Your biology is satisfied if you reproduce children, and they can be reproduced only by ejaculation, there is no need for orgasm.

Orgasm is a tremendous gift of nature. Man is deprived, and because he is so quick in making love the woman is also deprived. The woman needs time to warm up. Her whole body is erotic, and unless her whole body is throbbing with joy, she will not be able to experience orgasm. For that there is no time.

So for millions of years women have been completely denied their birthright. That's why they have become so bitchy, so continuously nagging, always ready to fight. There is no possibility of having a conversation with a woman. You are living with a woman for years, but there is not a single conversation that you can recall when you both were sitting together talking about great things of life. No, all that you will remember will be fighting, throwing things, being nasty! But the woman is not responsible for it. She's being deprived of her whole possibility of blissfulness. Then she becomes negative.

And this has given a chance to the priests. All the churches and the temples are filled up with women because they are the losers more than the men. Man's orgasm is more local; his whole body is not erotic, so his whole body does not suffer any damage if there is no orgasmic experience, but the woman's whole body suffers.

But it is good business for religions. Unless people are psychologically suffering, they will not come to the churches. They will not listen to all kinds of idiotic theologies. And because they are suffering, they want some consolation, they want some hope, at least after death. In life they know there is no hope; it is finished. This gives a chance to religions to show men and women both that sex is absolutely futile. It has no meaning, no significance. You are unnecessarily losing your energy, wasting your energy—and their argument seems to be correct because you have never experienced anything.

So by preventing the orgasmic experience, religions have made men and women slaves. Now the same slavery functions for other vested interests. The latest priest is the psychoanalyst; now he's exploiting the same thing. I was amazed to know that almost all new priests, particularly Christians, study psychology in their theological colleges. Psychology and psychoanalysis have become a necessary part of their education. Now what has psychology to do with the Bible? What has psychoanalysis to do with Jesus Christ? They are being trained in psychology and psychoanalysis because it is clear that the old priest is disappearing, losing his grip over people. The priest has to be brought up to date, so he can function not only as a religious priest but also as a psychoanalyst, psychologist. Naturally the psychologist cannot compete with him. He has something more: religion.

But this whole thing has happened through a simple device of condemning sex. So when in your therapy groups you find people fearing orgasm, help them to understand that orgasm is going to make you more sane, more intelligent, less angry, less violent, more loving. Orgasm is going to give you your roots which have been taken away from you. So don't be worried. And mixed into the fear in orgasm will be the fear that one may go crazy. If in orgasm one goes crazy, help him to go crazy! Only then he will be able to have it in its totality. But the orgasm relaxes every fiber of your mind, your heart, your body.

It is immensely important for meditation that a person has the experience of orgasm. Then you can help him understand what meditation is. It is an orgasmic experience with the whole existence. If the orgasm can be so beautiful and so beneficial, so healthy, with just a single human being, meditation is getting into oneness with the whole that surrounds you, from the smallest blade of grass to the biggest star, millions of years away.

Once he experiences this . . . The question is always the first experience. Once he knows it, that the craziness was not craziness but a kind of explosion of joy, and that cools down and leaves him healthier, more whole, more intelligent, then the fear of orgasm has disappeared. And with it he is finished with the religion, with the psychoanalysis, and all kinds of nonsense for which he is paying so tremendously.

The third fear you say is of death. The first is of being alone. Much of the fear of death will be destroyed by the first experience of being alone and having no fear. The remaining fear of death will be immediately destroyed by the experience of orgasm, because in the orgasm the person disappears. The ego is no more. There is an experiencing, but the experiencer is no more.

These first two steps will help to solve the third step very easily. And with each step you have to go on deepening the person's meditativeness. Any therapy without meditation cannot help much. It is just superficial, touching here and there, and soon the person will be the same again. A real transformation has never happened without meditation, and these are beautiful situations as far as meditation is concerned.

So use the first to make the person alone. Use the second to give him courage and tell him to drop all thoughts, just go crazily orgasmic: "Don't bother what happens. We are here to take care of you." With these two steps the third will be very easy. That is the easiest. It looks like the biggest fear of man—it is not true. You don't know death; how can you be afraid of it? You have always seen other people dying, you have never seen yourself dying. Who knows, maybe you are the exception, because there is no proof that you are going to die. Those who have died have given proof that they were mortals.

When I was in the university and learning logic from my professor, in every logic book, in every university around the world, the same Aristotelian syllogism is being taught: "Man is mortal. Socrates is a man. Therefore Socrates is mortal." And when I was taught that syllogism for the first time, I stood up and I said, "Wait. I may be the exception. Up to now I have been the exception. Why not tomorrow? About Socrates I accept the syllogism is true because he is dead, but what about me? What about you? What about all these people who are living? They have not died yet."

Experiencing death—people dying in disgust, in misery, in suffering, in all kinds of pain, old age—that gives you the fear of death. Nobody has known the death of an enlightened man, how beautifully he dies, how joyously he dies. The moment of his death is of tremendous luminosity, silence, as if joy is radiating from every pore of his being. Those who are near him, those who have been fortunate to be near him, will be simply surprised that death is far more glorious than life has ever been.

But this kind of death happens only to people who have lived totally, without fear, who have lived orgasmically, without bothering about idiots and what they are saying. They know nothing about it, and they go on talking about it.

The fear of death will be the simplest out of the three. You have to solve the first two, and then you tell the person that death is not the end of life. If you meditate deeply and reach to your innermost center you will suddenly find an eternal life current. The bodies . . . there have been many. There have been many forms to your being, but you are just the same. But it has to be not just a belief—it has to be made their experience.

So remember one thing: Your therapy groups should not be ordinary therapy—just somehow whitewashing and giving a man a feeling that he has learned something, he has experienced something and after a week or two he is the same. There is not a single person in the whole world who is totally psychoanalyzed. And there are thousands of psychoanalysts doing psychoanalysis, and not a single case they have been able to complete yet, for the simple reason because they have nothing to do with meditation. And without meditation you can go on painting on the surface, but the inner reality remains the same.

My therapists have to introduce meditation as the very center of therapy, and everything else should revolve around it. Then we have made therapy something really valuable. Then it is not only the need of those who are sick or of those who are somehow mentally unbalanced, or of those who feel fears, jealousies, violence. This is a negative part of therapy.

Our therapies should be that we give the person his individuality back. We give him his childhood and innocence back. That we give him integrity, crystallization, so that he never fears death. And once the fear of death disappears all other fears are very small, they will follow it, they will simply disappear.

And we have to teach people how to live totally and wholly, against the teachings of all the religions. They teach renounce. I teach rejoice.

Realities East and West

Western science knows only one reality—that of matter. It is poor, it lacks variety. The Eastern mysticism accepts the reality of your inner self—which you cannot see, cannot understand, but which you *are*. You can be awakened to it or you can remain asleep, it makes no difference to the inner quality of your being. That is your ultimate reality.

Then there is the body, which is only an appearance—an appearance in the sense that it is changing constantly. You see a beautiful woman or a beautiful man and they are already becoming old. The moment you rejoice in the beauty of a rose, the time for it to disappear back into the earth is not far away. This kind of reality has also its place in the Eastern vision. They call it appearance, moment to moment changing. There is a time to be born and there is a time to die. The seasons will come again, and the flowers will blossom again. It is the round trip of existence in which everything goes on changing except your being, your center. This changing world is a relative reality.

And then there are other realities—like dreams. You know they are not real, but still you see them. Not only do you see them, they affect you. If you have a nightmare and you wake up you will see that your heart is beating harder, your breathing is changed by the nightmare. You may even be perspiring out of fear. You cannot say that the nightmare is not there; otherwise from where has this perspiration come, this changed heartbeat and breathing? Eastern mysticism also accepts this third layer of reality: the dream, the horizon that you see all around, which exists nowhere but you can see it from everywhere.

So according to Eastern mysticism, everything passes and yet there is something that never passes; everything is born and dies and yet there is something that is never born and never dies. And unless you get centered in that eternal source you will not find peace, you will not find serenity. You will not find blissfulness, you will not find contentment. You will not feel at home, at ease in the universe. You will remain just an accident, you will never become essential.

The whole effort of any meditative method is to bring you closer to that which never changes, that which is always. It knows no time—if there is no change, how can there be a past, future, present? The world that knows past, future, and present can only be relatively real—today it is here, tomorrow it is gone. The body you had believed in so much one day dies. The mind you had believed in so much does not follow you, it dies with the body. It has been a part of the body mechanism.

That which flies out of the body in death is an invisible bird flying into an invisible sky. But if you are aware you will be dancing, because for the first time you will have known what freedom is. It is not a political freedom or an economic freedom; it is a more fundamental, existential freedom. And anything that grows out of this freedom is beautiful, graceful. Your eyes are the same but their vision has changed. Your love is there but it is no longer lust, it is no longer possessiveness. It transforms itself into compassion. You still share your joy in your songs, in your dances, in your poetry, in your music—but just for sheer joy.

It has been a centuries-long debate: What is art for? There have been pragmatic utilitarians who say that art should serve some purpose, otherwise it is useless. But these people don't know art. Art can only be for its own sake. It is the sheer joy of a solitary cuckoo, of the bamboos standing in silence, of a bird flying into the sky. Just the very flight, the very feel of freedom is enough unto itself. It need not serve anything else.

But that is possible only if you have known your fundamental existence.

You are acquainted with the mind, which is borrowed, which is nurtured, educated. You are acquainted with your body very superficially. You don't know how it functions, although it is your body. You don't know how it turns food into blood, how it distributes oxygen to different parts of the body. The body has its own wisdom. Nature has not left it to you to remember breathing, because you can forget. You are so sleepy, nature cannot take the risk.

If you had to remember breathing, I don't think you would have been here! You would have been forgotten long before.

But whether you remember or not, whether you are awake or asleep, the breathing continues on its own, the heart goes on working on its own, the stomach goes on digesting on its own. It does not ask your advice, nor does it need any medical education, nor does it need any advice. It has simply an intrinsic wisdom of its own.

But it is just your house—you are not it. This house is going to become, one day, old. One day its walls will start dropping away, its doors falling off. One day there will not be even a trace of the house; all will be gone. But what happened to the man who used to live in the house?

You have to understand that principle. You can call it awareness, enlightenment, consciousness, buddhahood—it doesn't matter what name you give to it. But it is the absolute responsibility of every human being not to waste time in mundane affairs. First things first! And the first thing is to be and to know what this being is. Don't go on running after butterflies. Don't go on looking at the horizon, which appears to be but is not.

I am reminded . . . Twenty-three centuries ago, Alexander the Great went to India. His teacher was a great philosopher, the father of logic, Aristotle. And when he was leaving for India, Aristotle asked him, "Can you bring something back for me as a gift?"

Alexander said, "Anything—just say it."

Aristotle said, "It is not so easy, but I will be waiting. Please bring me a sannyasin when you come back, a man who has realized himself. Because we don't know what this means . . . what it means to be a buddha. Get hold of a buddha and bring him back with you."

Alexander was not aware of what he was promising. He said, "Don't be worried. If Alexander wants to move the Himalayas, they will have to move. And you are asking only about a human being. Just wait—within a few months I will be back."

There was so much to do that Alexander remembered only at the last moment that he had forgotten to catch hold of a buddha, of one who knows the innermost reality. He inquired on the borders of India just as he was returning. People laughed at the very idea. They said, "In the first place, it is very difficult to recognize that somebody is a buddha. In the second place, if by chance you are open enough to receive the radiance of a buddha, you will fall at his feet. You will forget all about taking him with you. We hope that you don't find a buddha—just go back home."

Alexander could not understand. . . . What kind of human being is a buddha, that he cannot be taken away by force? Finally, he said: "Send messengers all over the place, find out if there is somebody who proclaims that he has arrived home."

His people came back and they said, "Yes, one naked sannyasin standing by the side of the river says, 'Where else can I be?—I am here. And who else can I be?—I am the buddha.'"

Alexander went himself to meet the man. The dialogue was tremendously beautiful, but very shocking to Alexander the Great. He had never come across such a man because before he said a single word—Alexander was holding a naked sword in his hand—the old man, naked, poor, said, "Put your sword back into its sheath, it will not be needed here. A man of intelligence carrying a sword? I will hit you! Just put the sword back into its sheath."

Alexander for the first time found somebody who could order him, and he had to follow. In spite of himself he had to follow.

And he said, "I have come with a prayer: Just come with me, to my land. My teacher wants to see a buddha. In the West we don't know anything about what this inner self means."

The old man laughed. He said, "This is hilarious. If your teacher does not know, he is not even a teacher. And if he wants to see a buddha, he will have to come to a buddha; a buddha cannot be carried to him. Just tell your teacher, 'If you are thirsty, come to the well; the well is not going to come to you.'"

"And as for you, Alexander," the old man said, "learn at least to be human. You introduced yourself as Alexander the Great. This is the ego that is preventing you from knowing your buddha. You are carrying it within yourself, but this 'greatness,' this desire to conquer the world . . . What will you accomplish by conquering the world? Soon death will take everything away. You will die naked, you will be buried in the earth. Nobody will even bother not to tread over you, and you will not be able to object, 'Keep away. I am Alexander the Great.' Please drop this idea of greatness. And also remember that even the word 'Alexander' is not your name."

Alexander asked him, "What do you mean it is not my name? Of course it is!"

The sannyasin said, "Nobody comes into the world with a name. All kinds of names are given—labels stuck upon you—and you become the label. You forget completely that you had come without any name, without any fame, and you will die in the same way.

"Tell your teacher to come here to face the lion. If he has the capacity to move inward, only then can he know what it means to be a buddha, what it means to be enlightened. Just by meeting somebody who is enlightened you cannot understand it—it is just like when somebody else drinks water it cannot quench your thirst."

Alexander touched the feet of the old man and said, "I am sorry to disturb you. Perhaps we don't understand each other's language at all."

And it is even today true: The Western mind and the Western-educated mind have forgotten the language of mysticism, of the East. You have to be very conscious, very alert, that you don't misunderstand. A different world, a different climate which used to exist, which had made this world a beautiful searching and seeking pilgrimage. . . . Now it is only a marketplace for purchasing arms, and fighting and killing and wars. Who bothers about meditation? It seems to be a very faraway echo. It does not seem to be related with us in any way. But unless you are open to this faraway echo, you will not understand.

It happened . . . A very learned scholar was blind, in the times of Gautam Buddha. And he was so articulate in debate and argumentation that the whole village was tortured by him, because everybody tried, "You are blind, that's why light is not within your reach."

But he said, "Then make it available through other sources. I can hear—beat it like a drum." You cannot beat light like a drum.

And the blind man said, "I can touch, at least let me touch light. My hand is open—where is your light? I can smell . . ." But none of these senses are capable of sensing the reality of light. The whole village was tortured: "What to do with this man? He is so argumentative . . . we all know what light is, but he denies its reality. And he has valid reasons—we cannot offer any proof."

They heard that Gautam Buddha was coming to their village.

They thought, "This is a good opportunity to take this blind man to Gautam Buddha. If Gautam Buddha cannot convince him then perhaps it is not possible. And either way it will be interesting; we can see how far Gautam Buddha can argue with this man."

But they were wrong. Gautam Buddha did not argue with the man. He simply said, "Don't harass him, it is ugly of you to tell him there is light. If you were compassionate enough you should have tried to find some physician to cure his eyes. Light is not an argument; you need eyes to see it and then there is no question of any doubt."

Buddha had his own personal physician traveling with him. He told his physician, "You remain in this village until this man's eyes are cured. I will be moving with my caravan."

After six months the physician and the blind man traveled to the place where Buddha was, and the man was no longer blind. He came dancing! He fell to the feet of Gautam Buddha and he said, "I am so grateful to you that you were not philosophical with me, that you did not humiliate me. That rather than engaging in a great debate you simply made a simple point: That it is not a question of light, it is a question of eyes."

The same is true about the inner self—it is not a question of your intelligence, not a question of your rationality, not a question of your logic, of your scientific knowledge, of your scriptures. It is a question of direct penetration with closed eyes into your own being, hidden behind your bones. Once that is known, a tremendous relaxation follows. Life for the first time becomes a dance. Even death is no longer a disturbance.

There is an ancient story . . . a very curious young fish is inquiring, "I have heard so much about the ocean but I don't see where it is."

An old fish said to the young philosopher, "Don't be an idiot—we are in the ocean, and we are the ocean. We come out of it and we disappear into it. We are nothing but waves in the ocean."

The same is true about the birds. Do you think they can find the sky? Although they are flying all the day—faraway places—they cannot find the sky. Because they are born out of the sky and one day they will disappear into the sky.

These are symbolic statements. They are in fact saying that you are part of the universe. You arise like a wave in the universe and you disappear one day back into the universe. This universe is not something objective, it is something subjective. It is something that is connected with your innermost core. If you have found yourself you have found the whole ocean, the whole sky, with all its stars, with all its flowers, with all its birds. To find oneself is to find everything. And to miss oneself . . . you may have palaces and empires and great riches—all is futile.

The fish and the birds are spontaneous beings. Except man, in this whole universe nobody has gone insane. You go on working even though there is no need to work—keep busy without any busyness, otherwise somebody will point to you and ask, "What are you doing?" You won't have the courage to say, "I am just being." People will laugh and they will suggest, "Do something, just being will not help. Get a job! Earn money." But a fish will not work more than is absolutely needed.

Henry Ford, before his death, was asked, "You have long before crossed the line, broken all records in terms of wealth. Now there is no competitor to you. Why do you go on working all the time?"

He used to come to his office at seven o'clock every morning. The office custodians used to come at eight o'clock, the clerks at nine, the managers at ten. The managers would be gone by four, the clerks would be gone by five, the custodians would be gone by six, but Henry Ford would be still working. And he was the richest man of his times.

The questioner was right to ask him, "Why do you go on and on and on? It is unnecessary activity. You have earned so much, you could do anything you wanted."

His answer was that of a wise man—not enlightened, but certainly life had made him wise. He said, "It just became a habit. I could not stop myself from working to become more and more rich. I knew it was not needed anymore, but it is very difficult to drop an old habit, a lifelong habit."

Except man . . . no trees have any habits, nor birds, nor fish. The whole of nature is spontaneous. It simply functions when it is needed, it stops functioning and remains simply silent when it is not needed. In fact, according to me this is sanity: To do only as much as is needed. Even to go a single inch further and you have moved beyond sanity, you have become insane. And there is no end to insanity.

This can be understood from many aspects. Except man, no animal is interested in sex all the year round. There is a season, a mating season. And once that season is gone, for the remainder of the year nobody bothers about sex. You will not find sex maniacs amongst birds, nor will you find celibates. You will not find, even in their mating season, that they are especially happy.

I have been watching birds, animals, and I am amazed that their sexual activity seems to be a thing forced on them. They don't look happy. Just look at a dog making love. He is doing it under some compulsion, some biological compulsion; otherwise he is not interested. And once the season is gone there is no interest at all. That's why marriage has not appeared in the animal world. What will you do with a marriage? Once the mating season ends—good-bye to each other!

But with man it is a habit. He has turned even a biological necessity into a habit. You will be surprised to know that according to psychologists and their surveys, every man is thinking about women at least once every four minutes, and every woman is thinking of men at least once every seven minutes. This disparity is the cause of tremendous misery.

That's why every night, when the husband comes home . . . the wife was perfectly okay, and suddenly she starts having a British face, she is suffering from a headache. Smart husbands bring aspirin home with them! But there are very rarely smart husbands, because if you are smart you will never be a husband. That kind of thing is for the unintelligent, the intelligent remain absolutely free.

If you watch humanity, you will not believe that this is not a madhouse. Somebody is smoking a cigarette . . . even though on the packet it is written it is dangerous to your life.

There are people who are chewing gum. One cannot think of a more idiotic thing. Chewing gum? Gum is made for chewing? People are doing all kinds of things that, if they watch and note them down, they will find . . . "My God, these things I am doing, and people still think me sane." But everybody is wearing a mask and trying to hide every insanity behind it. That is the whole purpose of Dynamic Meditation . . . it gives you the opportunity to put your mask away and let all the insanity of centuries come out. Don't hold it back, because it is a tremendous cleansing. And once you are a clean, clear consciousness your realization of buddhahood is not far away—perhaps just one step more.

Man's oceanic relationship with existence is completely broken, there is no bridge left. And this is what is making him do all kinds of stupid things. In three thousand years, five thousand wars. . . . One cannot believe that we are here just to kill each other! Isn't there anything more important than nuclear weapons? Seventy percent of the whole humanity's wealth goes into war efforts. Even the poor countries, where they cannot afford food twice a day for their people, where they are living under the poverty line, still they are wasting 70 percent of their income in creating bombs, in purchasing weapons. Do you think anything can be more insane than war?

A country like Germany, one of the most cultured, fell into the hands of a madman, Adolf Hitler. Nobody thinks about why it happened. Even a man like Martin Heidegger, perhaps the greatest philosopher in Germany, was a follower of Adolf Hitler. And Adolf Hitler was absolutely insane. He needed to be hospitalized.

But there must be something in every man to which he appealed. The whole of Germany, with all its intelligence, became a victim of that madman. And you can see the stupidity. He said, "It is because of the Jews that Germany is not rising as a world power, otherwise it is our birthright to rule over the world. It is because of the Jews."

Why did people become convinced that he was right about such a stupid thing, that the Jews were preventing Germany from becoming a great power? The Jews contributed wealth, intelligence, so many things to Germany. So why did all the remaining Germans become convinced? It was out of jealousy. The Jews were rich, the Jews were intelligent, the Jews were always on top in everything.

It is very dangerous to be successful in an insane world because everybody wants to kill you—on any grounds; right or wrong, it does not matter. The whole of Germany became convinced, not because there was any argument or reason in Adolf Hitler's statements; but because every German was jealous of the Jewish intelligence, their success, their wealth, their lifestyle. Because of this jealousy, Adolf Hitler persuaded even the most intelligent Germans to act like animals.

And now the weapons Adolf Hitler used are just toys for children. Since the Second World War, the technology has grown so much more sophisticated . . . and it is still in the hands of all kinds of politicians, and politicians are people who are psychologically sick. Just the very desire for power is sickness.

A healthy man wants to love—not to possess, not to dominate. A healthy man rejoices in life—he does not go begging for votes. It is the people who are suffering from deep inferiority who want to have some power, to prove to themselves and to others that they are superior. The really superior person does not care a thing about power. He knows his superiority, he lives his superiority. In his songs, in his dances, in his poetry, in his paintings, in his music he lives his superiority. Only the inferior ones are left for politics.

You may be aware of your buddhahood or not aware of your buddhahood—don't be worried. When the right time and the right season come you will blossom into a buddha. So just wait . . .

wait intelligently, wait without desire; enjoy waiting, make waiting itself a blissful silence, and whatever is your birthright is bound to flower. Nobody can prevent a bird from flying, nobody can prevent a cuckoo from singing, nobody can prevent a rose from blossoming. Who is preventing you from becoming buddhas? Except you, nobody is responsible for it.

If you go into your inner world and into your inner sky you will find an eternal eternity, a pilgrimage without any beginning and without any end . . . an immortality, a deathlessness, which suddenly transforms you totally without any effort, without any austerity, without torturing yourself. You are already what you want to be, just a small thing is missing—very small. Wake up! In your waking you are a buddha.

In your sleep you remain a buddha, but you are not aware of it. When one person becomes a buddha he knows that everybody else is a buddha. Somebody is sleeping, somebody is snoring, somebody is running after a woman, somebody is doing some other kind of stupidity—but buddhas are buddhas. Even if you are smoking a cigarette, it does not mean that you have lost your essentiality; it only shows your sleep and nothing else.

Letting go, relaxing, settling into yourself, the origin is regained.

Psychological vs. Physical

I'm not sure I'm afraid of death so much as I'm afraid of any illness and pain of old age that might lead up to it. How does one overcome the fear of physical pain?

Psychological pain can be dissolved, and *only* psychological pain can be dissolved. The other pain, the physical pain, is part of life and death; there is no way to dissolve it. But it never creates a problem. Have you ever observed? The problem exists only when you are *thinking* about it. If you think of old age you become afraid—but old people are not trembling. If you think of illness you become afraid—but when the illness has already happened there is no fear, there is no problem. One accepts it as a fact. The real problem is always psychological. The physical pain is part of life. When you start *thinking* about it, it is not physical pain at all, it has become psychological. You think about death and there is fear—but when death actually happens there is no fear. Fear is always about something in the future. Fear never exists in the present moment.

If you are going to the front in a war, you will be afraid, you will be very apprehensive. You will tremble, you will not be able to sleep; many nightmares will haunt you. But once you are on the front—ask the soldiers—once you are on the front, you forget all about it. Bullets may be passing overhead and you can enjoy your lunch; bombs may be falling and you can play cards.

Reality never comes as a problem; it is only the ideas about reality that create the problem. So the first thing to be understood is that if you can dissolve the psychological pain, no problem is left. Then you start living in the moment.

Psychological pain is of the past, of the future, never of the present. Mind never exists in the present. In the present, reality exists, not the mind. Mind exists in the past and the future, and in the past and future, reality does not exist. In fact, mind and reality never come across each other. They have never seen each other's face. Reality remains unknown to mind, and mind remains unknown to reality.

There is an old fable. . . .

Darkness approached God and said, "Enough is enough! Your sun goes on haunting me, chasing me. I can never rest; wherever I go to rest he is there, and I have to run away again. I have not done any wrong to him, this is unjust! I have come to you to get justice."

It was perfectly right; the complaint was valid. God called the sun and asked, "Why do you go on chasing this poor woman, darkness? What has she done to you?"

The sun said, "I don't know her at all, I have never seen her! You just bring her in front of me; only then can I say something. I don't remember ever having done any wrong to her, because I don't know her; we are not familiar. Nobody has ever introduced us to each other, we are not even acquainted. This is the first time I am hearing about this woman, this darkness. You bring her!"

The case remains pending because God could not bring darkness before the sun. They cannot exist together, they cannot encounter each other. Where darkness is, the sun cannot be; where the sun is, the darkness cannot be.

Exactly the same is the relationship between mind and reality. The psychology is the problem, reality never is a problem. You just dissolve your psychological problems—and they are dissolved by dissolving the center of them all, the ego. Once you don't think yourself separate from existence, problems simply evaporate as dewdrops disappear in the morning when the sun rises, not even leaving a trace behind. They simply disappear.

Physical pain will remain, but again I insist that it has never been a problem to anybody. If your leg is broken, it is broken. It is not a "problem." The problem is only in the imagination: "If my leg is broken, then what am I going to do? How am I to avoid it, or how am I to behave in such a way that my leg is never broken?" Now, if you become afraid about such things you cannot live, because your legs can be broken, your neck can be broken, your eyes can go blind, anything is possible. Millions of things are possible, and if you become obsessed with all these problems that are possible . . . I am not saying they are not possible, they are all possible. Whatever has happened to any human being, ever, can happen to you. Cancer can happen, TB can happen, death can happen; everything is possible. The human being is vulnerable. You can just go outside on the road and you can be hit by a car.

I am not saying don't go outside on the road. You can sit in your room and the roof can fall in! There is no way to save yourself totally and perfectly. You can stay lying down in your bed . . . but do you know that 97 percent of people die in a bed? That is the most dangerous place! Avoid it as much as you can; never go to bed because 97 percent of people die there. Even traveling by airplane is not so dangerous; it is more dangerous to be in bed. And remember, more people die in the night . . . so, keep trembling!

Then it is up to you. Then you will not be able to live at all.

Psychological problems are the only problems. You can become paranoid, you can become split, you can become paralyzed because of fear—but this has nothing to do with reality.

You see a blind man walking on the road perfectly well; blindness in itself is not a problem. You can see beggars with their legs deformed, their hands gone, and still laughing and gossiping with each other, still talking about women, making remarks, singing a tune.

Just watch life: Life is never a problem. We have a tremendous capacity to adjust to the *fact*, but we have no capacity to adjust to the future. Once you try to protect yourself and secure yourself in the future, then you will be in turmoil, in a chaos. You will start falling apart. Then there are millions of problems—problems and problems and problems. You cannot even commit suicide, because the poison may not be the right poison. Somebody may have mixed something into it; it may not be poison at all. You may take it and you will lie down and wait and wait and still death will not come.

Then everything creates a problem.

> *Mulla Nasruddin was going to commit suicide. He came across an astrologer on the street, and the astrologer said, "Mulla, wait. Let me see your hand."*
>
> *He said, "Why should I be concerned with astrology now? I am going to commit suicide! So there is no point; now there is no future."*
>
> *The astrologer said, "Wait. Let me see whether you can succeed or not."*

The future remains. You may not succeed, you may be prevented by the police, you may misfire the gun. There is no way to be certain about the future—not even about death, not even about suicide, what to say about life? Life is such a complex phenomenon; how can you be certain? Everything is possible and nothing is certain.

If you become afraid, this is just your psychology. Something has to be done to your mind. And if you understand me rightly, meditation is nothing but an effort to look at reality without the mind—because that is the only way to look at reality. If the mind is there it distorts, it corrupts reality. Drop the mind and see reality direct, immediate, face-to-face, and there is no problem. Reality has never created any problem for anybody. I am here, you are also here—I don't see a single problem. If I fall ill, I fall ill. What is there to be worried about? Why make a fuss about it? If I die, I die.

A problem needs space. In the present moment there is no space. Things only happen, there is no time to think about it. You can think about the past because there is distance; you can think about the future, there is distance. In fact, future and past are created just to give us space so that we can worry. And the more space you have, the more worry.

Now in cultures like India people are even more worried because they think about the next life, and the next, ad infinitum— "What is going to happen in the next life?" When a person is going to do something he does not think only about the consequences that are going to happen here and now, he thinks, "What karma am I going to gather for my future life?" Now he will become even more worried. The person in a culture like India has more space. How is he going to fill that space? He will fill it with more and more problems. Worry is a way to fill the empty space of the future.

Physical pain is not a problem—when it is there, it is there; when it is not there, it is not there. A problem arises when something is not there and you want it to be there, or when something is there and you don't want it to be there. Those kinds of problems are always psychological: "Why is this pain there?" Now this is all psychological. Who is to say why it is there? There is nobody to answer. Explanations can be given but those are not really answers.

Explanations are simple. It is very simple—pain is there because pleasure is there. Pleasure cannot exist without pain. If you want a life that is absolutely painless, then you will have to live a life that is absolutely pleasureless; they come together in one package. They are not two things really; they are one thing—not different, not separate, and cannot be separated.

That's what man has been doing through the centuries, separating, trying to somehow have all the pleasures of the world and not have any pain. But this is not possible. The more pleasures you have, the more pain also. The bigger the peak, the deeper will be the valley by the side. You want no valleys and big peaks? Then the peaks cannot exist; they can exist only with valleys. The valley is nothing but a situation in which a peak becomes possible. They are joined together.

You want pleasure and you don't want pain. For example, you love a woman or you love a man, and when the woman is with you, you are happy. Now, you would like to be happy whenever she is with you, but when she goes away you don't want the pain. If you are really happy with a woman when she is with you, how can you avoid the pain of separation when she is gone? You will miss her, you will feel the absence. The absence is bound to become pain. If you really want not to have any pain, then you should avoid all pleasure. Then, when the woman is there don't feel happy; just remain sad, just remain unhappy so that when she goes, there is no problem. If somebody greets you and you feel happy, then when somebody insults you, you will feel unhappy. This trick has been tried.

This has been one of the most basic tricks that all of the so-called religious people have tried: if you want to avoid pain, avoid pleasure. But then what is the point? If you want to avoid death, avoid life—but then what is the point of it all? You will be dead. Before death, you will be dead. If you want to be perfectly secure, enter into your grave and lie down there and you will be perfectly secure! Don't breathe, because if you breathe there is danger—there are all sorts of infections, a million diseases exist all around you; how can you breathe? The air is polluted, there is danger. So don't breathe, don't move . . . just don't live. Commit suicide; then there will be no pain. But then why are you searching for it? You want no pain and all pleasure? You demand something impossible; you want two plus two not to be four. You want them to become five, or three, or anything else but four. But they *are* four. Whatever you do, however you try to deceive yourself and others, they will remain four.

Pain and pleasure go together like night and day, like birth and death, like love and hate. In a better world, with a more developed language, we will not use words like hate and love, anger and compassion, day and night. We will create some words that carry both together: *lovehate*—one word—*daynight*—one word, not two—*birthdeath*—one word, not two—*painpleasure*—one word, not two.

The language creates an illusion. In language, pain is separate from pleasure. If you want to look in the dictionary for *pain*, you have to look for *pain*—*pleasure* will be separate. But in reality, pain and pleasure are together just as your right and left hands are together, just as two wings of a bird are together. The dictionary creates an illusion; language is a very great source of illusions. It says "love" and when it says "love" you never think about hate. You completely forget about hate—but love cannot exist without hate. That's why you love a person and you hate the same person.

Never be uneasy about it. If you love, you will hate too. There will be moments when the hate part will be on top; there will be moments when the love part will be on top. Don't be uneasy about it; it is natural and human. You would like a world where coldness exists without anything like heat, or heat exists without anything like cold. Just think about it; it is absurd because heat and cold are together. And it depends on what you call them.

You can put water in two buckets: in one, hot water, boiling, and in the other, cold, ice-cold water. Just put both your hands into them, and just feel. Are there two sensations? Or is it one spectrum? At one extreme is cold, at the other extreme is hot. Then let them settle. By and by you will see that they are coming closer and closer; the hot is becoming less hot, and the cold is becoming less cold. After a few hours you will say, "They are both the same now." Or you can try an experiment in one bucket of water—put one hand near a heat source and one hand in ice water. Make one hand cold and one hot, and then dip both hands into the same bucket of water and feel what it is. One hand will say it is cold and one hand will say it is hot, but it is the same water. It's relative. Something may look like pleasure to you, and the same thing may look like pain to somebody else.

For example you are making love to a woman; you think it is very pleasurable. Ask a monk, and he will be simply horrified: "What are you doing? Have you gone mad?" Maybe that's why people make love in private—otherwise people will laugh and ridicule them; all the movements of lovemaking will look absurd, ridiculous. In a passionate state of mind, you are almost drunk.

When you are angry you do something; in that moment it gives you pleasure, otherwise you wouldn't do it. Anger gives tremendous pleasure, power, the feeling of power. But when the anger is gone you start feeling repentance, remorse. You start feeling that it was not good, now it is painful. When it was there you felt powerful and you felt pleasure. Now, in a less feverish state, you look again. You are cool and collected now; now it looks painful. A thing can be pleasurable, the same thing can be painful—it depends. And the same thing can be pleasurable to you and for somebody else can be painful—that too depends. Pleasure and pain go together.

My suggestion is that when there is pain, go deeply into it, don't avoid it. Let it be so, be open to it; become as sensitive as possible. Let the pain and its arrow penetrate you to your very core. Suffer it. And when the pleasure comes, let that too move you to your innermost core. Dance it.

When there is pain, be with pain, and when there is pleasure be with pleasure. Become so totally sensitive that each moment of pain and pleasure is a great adventure. If you can do this, you will understand that pain too is beautiful. It is as beautiful as pleasure. It also brings a sharpness to your being; it also brings awareness to your being—sometimes even more than pleasure. Pleasure dulls; that's why people who live just in indulgence will be found to be shallow. You will not see any depth in them. They have not known pain at all; they have lived only on the surface, moving from one pleasure to another. The "playboys" . . . they don't know what pain is.

Pain makes you very alert, and pain makes you compassionate, sensitive to others' pains too. Pain makes you immense, huge, big. The heart grows because of pain. It is beautiful, it has its own beauty. And I am not saying seek pain; I am only saying that whenever it is there, enjoy that too. It is a gift of existence and there must be a hidden treasure in it. Enjoy that too; don't reject. Accept it, welcome it, be with it. In the beginning it will be difficult, arduous. But by and by you will learn the taste of it.

When you start anything new, you have to learn the taste. And of course the taste of pain is bitter, but once you have learned it, it gives such sharpness and brilliance to you. It shakes all dust, all stupor and sleepiness from you. It makes you fully mindful in a way that nothing else can. In pain you can be more meditative than in pleasure. Pleasure is more distracting. Pleasure engulfs you; in pleasure you abandon consciousness. Pleasure is a sort of oblivion, a forgetfulness. Pain is a remembrance; you cannot forget pain.

Pain can become a very creative energy; it can become meditation, it can become awareness.

When pain is there, use it as awareness, as meditation, as a sharpening of the soul. And when pleasure is there, then use it as a drowning, as a forgetfulness.

Both are ways to reach your home. One is to remember yourself totally, and one is to forget yourself totally. Pain and pleasure both can be used, but to use them you have to be very, very intelligent. What I am teaching is not a stupid person's way; what I am teaching is for the intelligent, it is the way of the wise. Whatsoever existence gives you, try to find a way to use it in such a way that it becomes a creative growth situation for you.

Known vs. Unknown

Sometimes I have the feeling that my fear of death is really based in a fear of the unknown, because I don't know what will happen to me when I die. Can you say something about it?

Once you know what life is you will know what death is. Death is also part of the same process. Ordinarily we think death comes at the end, ordinarily we think death is against life, ordinarily we think death is the enemy, but death is not the enemy. And if you think of death as the enemy it simply shows that you have not been able to know what life is.

Death and life are two polarities of the same energy, of the same phenomenon—the tide and the ebb, the day and the night, the summer and the winter. They are not separate and not opposites, not contrary; they are complementary. Death is not the end of life; in fact, it is a completion of one life, the crescendo of one life, the climax, the finale. And once you know your life and its process, then you understand what death is.

Death is an organic, integral part of life, and it is very friendly to life. Without it life cannot exist. Life exists because of death; death gives the background. Death is, in fact, a process of renewal. And death happens each moment. The moment you breathe in and the moment you breathe out, both happen. Breathing in, life happens; breathing out, death happens. That's why when a child is born the first thing he does is breathe in, then life starts. And when an old man is dying, the last thing he does is breathe out, then life departs. Breathing out is death, breathing in is life—they are like two wheels of a bullock cart. You live by breathing out as much as you live by breathing in. The breathing out is part of breathing in; you cannot breathe in if you stop breathing out. You cannot live if you stop dying. The man who has understood what his life is allows death to happen; he welcomes it. He dies each moment and each moment he is resurrected. His cross and his resurrection are continually happening as a process. He dies to the past each moment and he is born again and again into the future.

If you look into life you will be able to know what death is. If you understand what death is, only then are you able to understand what life is. They are organic. Ordinarily, out of fear, we have created a division. We think that life is good and death is bad. We think that life has to be desired and death is to be avoided. We think somehow we have to protect ourselves against death. This absurd idea creates endless miseries in our lives, because a person who protects himself against death becomes incapable of living. He is the person who is afraid of exhaling—then he cannot inhale and he is stuck. Then he simply drags; his life is no longer a flow, his life is no longer a river.

If you really want to live you have to be ready to die. Who is afraid of death in you? Is life afraid of death? It is not possible. How can life be afraid of its own integral process? Something else is afraid in you. The ego is afraid in you. Life and death are not opposites, ego and death are opposites. Life and death are not opposites, ego and life are opposites. Ego is against both life and death. The ego is afraid to live and the ego is afraid to die. It is afraid to live because each effort, each step toward life, brings death closer.

If you live you are coming closer to dying. The ego is afraid to die, hence it is afraid to live also. The ego simply drags.

There are many people who are neither alive nor dead. This is worse than anything. A man who is fully alive is full of death also. That is the meaning of Jesus on the cross. Jesus carrying his own cross has not really been understood. And he says to his disciples, "You will have to carry your own cross." The meaning of Jesus carrying his own cross is very simple, nothing but this: Everybody has to carry his death continuously, everybody has to die each moment, everybody has to be on the cross because that is the only way to live fully, totally.

Whenever you come to a total moment of aliveness, suddenly you will see death there also. In love it happens. In love, life comes to a climax—hence people are afraid of love.

I have been continually surprised by people who come to me and say they are afraid of love. What is the fear of love? It is because when you really love somebody your ego starts slipping and melting. You cannot love with the ego; the ego becomes a barrier, and when you want to drop the barrier the ego says, "This is going to be a death. Beware!"

The death of the ego is not your death; the death of the ego is really your possibility of life. The ego is just a dead crust around you, it has to be broken and thrown away. It comes into being naturally—just as when a traveller passes, dust collects on his clothes, on his body, and he has to take a bath to get rid of the dust.

As we move in time, dust of experiences, of knowledge, of lived life, of past, collects. That dust becomes our ego. Accumulated, it becomes a crust around you which has to be broken and thrown away. One has to take a bath continuously—every day, in fact every moment, so that this crust never becomes a prison. The ego is afraid to love because in love, life comes to a peak. But whenever there is a peak of life there is also a peak of death—they go together.

In love you die and you are reborn.

Let it be remembered that death and life both become aflame together, they are never separate. If you are very, very minimally alive, at the minimum, then you can see death and life as being separate. The closer you come to the peak, the closer they start coming. At the very apex they meet and become one. In love, in meditation, in trust, in prayer, wherever life becomes total, death is there. Without death, life cannot become total.

But the ego always thinks in divisions, in dualities; it divides everything. Existence is indivisible; it cannot be divided. You were a child, then you became a youth; can you demark the point in time where suddenly you were no longer a child and you had become a youth? One day you become old. Can you demark the line when you become old?

Processes cannot be demarked. Exactly the same happens when you are born. Can you demark when you are born, or when life really starts? Does it start when the child starts breathing—the doctor spanks the child and the child starts breathing? Is life born then? Or is it when the child got into the womb, when the mother became pregnant, when the child was conceived? Does life start then? Or, even before that? When does life start, exactly?

It is a process of no ending and no beginning. It never starts. When is a person dead? Is a person dead when the breathing stops? Many yogis have now proved on scientific grounds that they can stop breathing and they are still alive and they can come back. So the stopping of the breathing cannot be the end. Where does life end?

It never ends anywhere, it never begins anywhere. We are involved in eternity. We have been here since the very beginning—if there was any beginning—and we are going to be here to the very end, if there is going to be any end. In fact, there cannot be any beginning and there cannot be any end. We are life—even if forms change, bodies change, minds change. What we call life is just an identification with a certain body, with a certain mind, with a certain attitude, and what we call death is nothing but getting out of that form, out of that body, out of that concept.

You change houses. If you get too identified with one house, then changing the house will be very painful. You will think that you are dying because the old house was what you were—that was your identity. But this doesn't happen, because you know that you are only changing the house, you remain the same. Those who have looked within themselves, those who have found who they are, come to know an eternal, nonending process. Life is a process, timeless, beyond time. Death is part of it.

Death is a continuous revival: a help to life to resurrect again and again, a help to life to get rid of old forms, to get rid of dilapidated buildings, to get rid of old confining structures so that again you can flow and you can again become fresh and young, and you can again become virgin.

I have heard:

A man was browsing through an antique shop near Mount Vernon and ran across a rather ancient-looking axe.

"That's a mighty old axe you have there," he said to the shop owner.

"Yes," said the man, "it once belonged to George Washington."

"Really?" said the customer. "It certainly stood up well."

"Of course," said the antique dealer, "it has had three new handles and two new heads."

But that's how life is—it goes on changing handles and heads; in fact, it seems that everything goes on changing and yet something remains eternally the same. Just watch. You were a child—what has remained of that now? Just a memory. Your body has changed, your mind has changed, your identity has changed. What has remained of your childhood? Nothing has remained, just a memory. You cannot make a distinction between whether it really happened, or you saw a dream, or you read it in a book, or somebody told you about it. Was the childhood yours or somebody else's? Sometimes have a look at the album of old photographs. Just see, this was you. You will not be able to believe it, you have changed so much. In fact everything has changed—handles and heads and everything! But still, deep down somewhere, something remains a continuity; a witnessing remains continuous. There is a thread, howsoever invisible, and everything goes on changing but that invisible thread remains the same.

That thread is beyond life and death. Life and death are two wings for that which is beyond life and death. That which is beyond goes on using life and death as two wheels of a cart, complementary. It lives through life; it lives through death. Death and life are its processes, like inhalation and exhalation. But something in you is transcendental.

But we are too identified with the form—that creates the ego. That's what we call "I." Of course the "I" has to die many times. So it is constantly in fear, trembling, shaking, always afraid, protecting, securing.

A Sufi mystic knocked at the door of a very rich man. He was a beggar and he wanted nothing but enough to have a meal.

The rich man shouted at him and said, "Nobody knows you here!"

"But I know myself," said the dervish. "How sad it would be if the reverse were true. If everybody knew me but I was not aware of who I was, how sad it would be. Yes, you are right, nobody knows me here, but I know myself."

These are the only two situations possible, and you are in the sad situation. Everybody may know about you, who you are, but you yourself are completely oblivious of your transcendence, of your real nature, of your authentic being. This is the only sadness in life. You can find many excuses, but the real sadness is this: You don't know who you are.

How can a person be happy not knowing who he is, not knowing from where he comes, not knowing where he is going? A thousand and one problems arise because of this basic self-ignorance.

A bunch of ants came out of the darkness of their underground nest in search of food. It was early in the morning. The ants happened to pass by a plant whose leaves were covered with morning dew.

"What are these?" asked one of the ants, pointing to the dewdrops. "Where do they come from?"

Some said, "They come from the earth."

Others said, "They come from the sea."

Soon a quarrel broke out—there was a group who adhered

to the sea theory, and a group who attached themselves to the earth theory.

Only one, a wise and intelligent ant, stood alone. He said, "Let us pause a moment and look around for signs, for everything has an attraction toward its source. And, as it is said, everything returns to its origin. No matter how far into the air you throw a brick it comes down to the earth. Whatever leans toward the light, must originally be of the light."

The ants were not totally convinced yet and were about to resume their dispute, but the sun had come up and the dewdrops were leaving the leaves, rising, rising toward the sun and disappearing into it.

Everything returns to its original source, has to return to its original source. If you understand life then you understand death also. Life is a forgetfulness of the original source, and death is again a remembrance. Life is going away from the original source, death is coming back home. Death is not ugly, death is beautiful. But death is beautiful only for those who have lived their life unhindered, uninhibited, unsuppressed. Death is beautiful only for those who have lived their life beautifully, who have not been afraid to live, who have been courageous enough to live—who loved, who danced, who celebrated.

Death becomes the ultimate celebration if your life is a celebration.

Let me tell you in this way: Whatsoever your life was, death reveals it. If you have been miserable in life, death reveals misery. Death is a great revealer. If you have been happy in your life, death reveals happiness. If you have lived only a life of physical comfort and physical pleasure, then of course, death is going to be very uncomfortable and very unpleasant, because the body has to be left.

The body is just a temporary abode, a shrine in which we stay for the night and leave in the morning. It is not your permanent abode, it is not your home. So if you have lived just a bodily life and you have never known anything beyond the body, death is going to be very, very ugly, unpleasant, painful. Death is going to be an anguish. But if you have lived a little higher than the body, if you have loved music and poetry, and you have loved, and you have looked at the flowers and the stars, and something of the nonphysical has entered into your consciousness, death will not be so bad, death will not be so painful. You can take it with equanimity—but still, it cannot be a celebration.

If you have touched something of the transcendental in yourself, if you have entered your own nothingness at the center—the center of your being, where you are no longer a body and no longer a mind, where physical pleasures are completely left far away and mental pleasures such as music and poetry and literature and painting, everything, are left far away, you are simply just pure awareness, consciousness—then death is going to be a great celebration, a great understanding, a great revelation.

If you have known anything of the transcendental in you, death will reveal to you the transcendental in the universe—then death is no longer a death but a meeting with the source, a date with the divine.

Afraid of Life

You've touched on something that rings a bell for me—if I look into it, I feel that I'm really more afraid of life than I am of death. Can you say more about how these fears are related?

One who is afraid of death will be afraid of life also, because life brings death. If you are afraid of the enemy and you blockade your door, the friend will also be prohibited from entering. You are so afraid the enemy may enter that you blockade the door for the friend also. You become so afraid that you cannot even open the door for a friend, because who knows? The friend may turn out to be an enemy. Or, when the door is open for the friend the enemy may enter too.

People have become afraid of life because they are afraid of death. They don't live—because at the highest points, the peaks, death always penetrates into life. Have you watched this happening? So many women have lived a frigid life, afraid of orgasm, afraid of that wild explosion of energy. For centuries women have been frigid; they have not known what orgasm is. And the majority of men suffer because of that fear too—95 percent of men suffer from premature ejaculation. They are so afraid of orgasm, there is so much fear that somehow they want to finish it, somehow they want to get out of it. Again and again they go into lovemaking and there is fear. The woman remains frigid and the man becomes so afraid that he cannot stay in that state any longer. The very fear makes him ejaculate sooner than is natural, and the woman remains closed, holding herself back.

The very possibility for orgasm disappears when there is so much fear. In the deepest orgasm death penetrates; you feel as if you are dying. If a woman goes into orgasm she starts moaning, she starts crying, screaming. She may even start saying, "I am dying. Don't kill me!" That actually happens: "I am dying! Don't kill me, stop!" A moment comes in deep orgasm where ego cannot exist, and death penetrates. But that is the beauty of orgasm.

People have become afraid of love because in love also, death penetrates. If two lovers are sitting side-by-side in deep love and intimacy, not even talking . . . Talking is an escape, an escape from love. When two lovers are talking that simply shows they are avoiding intimacy. The words in between them give distance—with no words, distance disappears and death appears. In silence, death is there, just lurking around—a beautiful phenomenon! But people are so afraid that they go on talking whether it is needed or not. They go on talking about anything and everything, but they cannot keep silent.

If two lovers sit silently, death suddenly surrounds them. And when two lovers are silent you will see a certain happiness and also a certain sadness—happiness because life is at its peak, and sadness because at the peak of life, death also comes in. Whenever you are silent you will feel a sort of sadness. Even looking at a rose flower, if you are sitting silently and not saying anything about the rose flower, just looking at it, in that silence you will suddenly feel it is there—death. You will see the flower withering, within moments it will be gone, lost forever. Such a beauty and so fragile! Such a beauty and so vulnerable! Such a beauty, such a miracle and soon it will be lost forever and it will not return again. Suddenly you will become sad.

Whenever you meditate you will find death moving around you. In love, in orgasm, in any aesthetic experience—in music, in song, in poetry, in dance—wherever you suddenly lose your ego, death is there.

So let me tell you one thing. You are afraid of life because you are afraid of death. And I would like to teach you how to die so that you lose all fear of death. The moment you lose the fear of death you become capable of living.

And don't misunderstand me. I am not talking against life. How can I talk against life? I am madly in love with life, I am so madly in love with life that because of it I have fallen in love with death also. It is part of life—when you love life totally, how can you avoid death? You have to love death also. When you love a flower deeply, you love its withering away also. When you love a woman deeply, you love her getting old also, you one day love her death also. That is part of her life, part of the woman. Old age has not happened from the outside, it has come from the inside. The beautiful face has become wrinkled now—you love those wrinkles also, they are part of your woman. You love a man and his hair has grown white—you love those hairs also. They have not happened from the outside; they are not accidents. Life is unfolding and now the black hair has disappeared and the gray hair has come. You don't reject the gray hairs, you love them, they are a part of the man. Then your man becomes old, becomes weak—you love that too. Then one day the man is gone—you love that too.

Love loves all. Love knows nothing else than love. Hence I say love death. If you can love death it will be very simple to love life. If you can love even death, there is no problem. The problem arises because you have been repressing something, because you are afraid of life. Then repression brings about dangerous outcomes. If you go on repressing and repressing, one day you will lose all aesthetic sense. You lose all sense of beauty, sense of grace, sense of divinity. Then the very repression becomes such a feverish state that you can do anything that is ugly.

Let me tell you a beautiful anecdote. A friend has sent it who always sends beautiful jokes!

> *This marine is sent to a distant island outpost where there are no women, but there is a large monkey population. He is shocked to see that without exception his fellow marines all make love with the monkeys. And he swears to them that he will never get that horny. They tell him not to be closed-minded. But as the months passed by, the marine can hold out no longer. He grabs the first monkey he can and gets caught in the act by his buddies, who start laughing their heads off.*
>
> *Surprised, he says to them, "What are you guys laughing at? You keep telling me to do it!"*
>
> *They answer, "Yeah, but did you have to pick the ugliest one?"*

If you repress, the possibility is that you may choose the ugliest life. Then the very fever is so much that you are not in your consciousness. Then you are almost in a neurosis. Before the repression becomes too much, relax, move into life. It is your life! Don't feel guilty. It is your life to live and love and to know and be. And whatever instincts nature has given to you, they are just indications of where you have to move, where you have to seek, where you have to find your fulfillment.

I know that this material life of the body is not all—a greater life is hidden behind it. But it is hidden *behind* it. You cannot find that greater life by going against this life; you can find that greater life only by indulging deeply in this life. There are waves on the ocean—the ocean is hidden just behind the waves. If, seeing the turmoil and the chaos you escape from the waves, you will be escaping from the ocean and its depths also. Jump in, those waves are part of it. Dive deep and the waves will disappear, and then there will be the depth and the absolute silence of the ocean.

3

UNCERTAIN AND UNKNOWN— THE MYSTERY OF TRUST

Life can be known, death also—but nothing can be said about them. No answer will be true; it cannot be by the very nature of things. Life and death are the deepest mysteries. It would be better to say that they are not two mysteries, but two aspects of the same mystery, two doors of the same secret. But nothing can be said about them. Whatever you say, you will miss the point.

Life can be lived, death also can be lived. They are experiences—one has to pass through them and know them. Nobody can answer your questions. How can life be answered? Or death? Unless *you* live, unless *you* die, who's going to answer?

But many answers have been given—and remember, all answers are false. There is nothing to choose. It is not that one answer is correct and other answers are incorrect; all answers are incorrect. There is nothing to choose. Experience, not answers, can answer.

So this is the first thing to be remembered when you are near a real mystery, not a riddle created by man. If it is a riddle created by man it can be answered, because then it is a game, a mind game— you create the question, you create the answer. But if you are facing something which you have not created, how can you answer it, how can the human mind answer it? It is incomprehensible for the human mind. The part cannot comprehend the whole. The whole can be comprehended by *becoming* whole. You can jump into it and be lost—and there will be the answer.

I will tell you one anecdote that Ramakrishna loved to tell.

Once it happened that there was a great festival near a sea, on the beach. Thousands of people were gathered there and suddenly they all became engrossed in a question—whether the sea is immeasurable or measurable. Whether there is a bottom to it or not; is it fathomable or unfathomable? By chance, one man completely made of salt was also there. He said, "You wait, and you discuss, and I will go into the ocean and find out, because how can one know unless one goes into it?"

So the man of salt jumped into the ocean. Hours passed, days passed, then months passed, and people started to go to their homes. They had waited long enough, and the man of salt was not coming back.

The man of salt, the moment he entered the ocean, started melting, and by the time he reached the bottom he was not. He came to know—but he couldn't come back. And those who didn't know, they discussed it for a long time. They may have arrived at some conclusions, because the mind loves to reach conclusions.

Once a conclusion is reached, the mind feels at ease—hence so many philosophies exist. All philosophies exist to fulfill a need:

The mind asks and the mind cannot remain with the question, it is uneasy; to remain with the question feels inconvenient. An answer is needed—even if it is false it will do; mind is put at rest.

To go and take a jump into the sea is dangerous. And remember, we are all men of salt as far as the ocean is concerned—the ocean of life and death. We are men of salt, and we will melt into it because we come from it. We are made by it, we are of it. We will melt!

So the mind is always afraid of going into the ocean—it is made of salt, it is bound to dissolve. It is afraid, so it remains on the shore discussing things, debating, arguing, creating theories—all false, because they are based on fear. A courageous person will take the jump, and will resist accepting any answer which is not known and experienced by himself.

We are cowards, that's why we accept anyone else's answer. Mahavira, Buddha, Christ—we accept their answers. But their answers cannot be our answers. Nobody else's knowledge can be yours—they may have known, but their knowledge is just information for you. *You* will have to know. Only when it is your own is it knowledge. Otherwise it will not give you wings; on the contrary, it will hang around your neck like a stone, you will become a slave to it. You will not achieve liberation, you will not be set free by it.

Says Jesus, "Truth liberates." Have you seen anybody being liberated by theories? Experience liberates, yes . . . but theories about experience? No, never!

But the mind is afraid to take the jump, because mind is made of the same stuff as the universe; if you take the jump you will be lost. You will come to know, but you will know only when you are not. The salt man came to know. He touched the very depths, he reached the very center, but he couldn't come back.

And even if he could, how would he relate . . . ? Even if he comes back, his language will belong to the center, to the depths, and your language belongs to the shore, to the periphery. There is no possibility of any communication. He cannot say anything meaningful, he can only remain silent—meaningfully, significantly. If he says something he himself will feel guilty, because he will immediately know that whatsoever he knows has not been transferred through the words; his experience is left behind. Only words have gone to you, dead, stale, empty.

Words can be communicated but not truth. Truth can only be indicated. The salt man can say to you, "You also come"—he can give you an invitation—"and take a jump with me into the ocean."

But you are very clever. You will say, "First answer the question; otherwise how do I know that you are right? Let me first consider and think and brood and ponder, then I will follow. When my mind is convinced, then I will take the jump."

But mind is never convinced, cannot be convinced. Mind is nothing but a process of doubt; it can never be convinced, it can go on arguing infinitely because whatever you say it can create an argument around it.

From Knowledge to Innocence

Don't become more knowledgeable, become more innocent. Drop all that you know, forget all that you know. Remain wondering, but don't transform your wondering into questions, because once the wonder is changed into a question, sooner or later the question will bring knowledge. And knowledge is a false coin.

From the state of wonder, there are two paths. One is of questioning—the wrong path—it leads you into more and more knowledge. The other is not of questioning but enjoying. Enjoy the wonder, the wonder that life is, the wonder that existence is, the wonder of the sun and the sunlight and the trees bathed in its golden rays. Experience it. Don't put in a question mark, let it be as it is.

Remain innocent, childlike, if you ever want a communion with existence and reality. Remain in wonder if you want the mysteries to open up for you. Mysteries never open up for those who go on questioning. Questioners sooner or later end up in a library. Questioners sooner or later end up with scriptures, because scriptures are full of answers.

And answers are dangerous, they kill your wonder. They are dangerous because they give you the feeling that you know, although you know not. They give you this misconception about yourself that now questions have been solved. "I know what the Bible says, I know what the Koran says, I know what the Gita says. I have arrived." You will become a parrot; you will repeat things but you will not know anything. This is not the way to know—knowledge is not the way to know.

Then what is the way to know? Wonder. Let your heart dance with wonder. Be full of wonder: Throb with it, breathe it in, breathe it out.

Why be in such a hurry for the answer? Can't you allow a mystery to remain a mystery? I know there is a great temptation not to allow it to remain a mystery, to reduce it to knowledge. Why is this temptation there? Because only if you are full of knowledge will you be in control.

Mystery will control you, knowledge will make you the controller. Mystery will possess you. You cannot possess the mysterious; it is so vast and your hands are so small. It is so infinite, you cannot possess it, you will have to be possessed by it—and that is the fear. Knowledge you can possess, it is so trivial; knowledge you can control.

This temptation of the mind to reduce every wonder, every mystery, to a question, is basically fear-oriented. We are afraid, afraid of the tremendousness of life, of this incredible existence. We are afraid. Out of fear we create some small knowledge around ourselves as a protection, as an armor, as a defense.

It is only cowards who reduce the tremendously valuable capacity of wondering to questions. The really brave, the courageous person, leaves it as it is. Rather than changing it into a question, he jumps into the mystery. Rather than trying to control it, he allows the mystery to possess him.

And the joy of being possessed, and the benediction of being possessed, is invaluable. You cannot imagine what it is, you have never dreamt about it—because to be possessed by the mystery is to be possessed by the whole.

Trusting the Inner Voice

When I listen to my inner voice, it tells me what I need sometimes is just to do nothing, just to sleep, eat, play on the beach. But I am afraid to follow these feelings because I think I will get too weak to survive in this world. Will existence really protect me if I just allow myself to let go?

The first thing is that there is no need to survive in this world. This world is a madhouse! There is no need to survive in it.

There is no need to survive in the world of ambition, politics, ego. It is the disease. But there is another way to be, and that is that you can be in this world and not be *of* it.

"When I listen to my inner voice it tells me what I need sometimes is just to do nothing. . . ." Then don't do anything! There is nobody higher than you, and existence speaks to you directly. Start trusting your inner feelings. Then don't do anything. If you feel just to sleep, eat, and play on the beach, perfect—let that be your religion! Don't be afraid.

You will have to drop fear. And if it is a question of choosing between the inner feeling and the fear, choose the inner feeling. Don't choose the fear. So many people have chosen their religion out of fear, so they live in a limbo. They are neither religious nor worldly; they live in indecision.

Fear is not going to help. Fear always means the fear of the unknown. Fear always means the fear of death. Fear always means the fear of being lost. But if you really want to be alive, you have to accept the possibility of being lost. You have to accept the insecurity of the unknown, the discomfort and the inconvenience of the unfamiliar, the strange. That is the price one has to pay for the blessing that follows it, and nothing can be achieved without paying for it. You have to pay for it; otherwise you will remain paralyzed by fear. Your whole life will be lost.

Enjoy whatsoever your inner feeling is.

"I think I will get too weak to survive in this world." There is no need. This is fear speaking in you, fear creating more fears. Out of fear more fear is born.

"Will existence really protect me?" Again the fear is asking for guarantees, promises. Who is there to give you a guarantee? Who can be a guarantee for your life? You are asking for some sort of insurance. No, there is no possibility. In existence, nothing is ensured—nothing can be. And it is good! Otherwise, if existence is also ensured, you will be already completely dead. Then the whole thrill of it, of being alive like a young leaf in the strong wind, will be lost.

Life is beautiful because it is insecure. Life is beautiful because there is death. Life is beautiful because it can be missed. If you cannot miss it, everything is forced upon you, then even life becomes an imprisonment. You will not be able to enjoy it. Even if you are ordered to be blissful, commanded to be free, then bliss and freedom both are gone.

"Will existence really protect me if I just allow myself to let go?" Try it and see! Only one thing I can say to you . . . I am not talking to your fear, remember. Only one thing I can say to all of you, and that is that those who have tried have found that existence protects. But I am not talking to your fear. I am simply encouraging your adventure, that's all. I am persuading, seducing you toward adventure. I am not talking to your fear. All those who have tried have found that the protection is infinite.

But I don't know whether you can understand the protection that the universe gives to you. The type of protection you are asking for cannot be given by the universe because you don't know what you are asking. You are asking for death. Only a dead body is absolutely protected. Something alive is always in danger. To be alive is a hazard. The more alive the more adventure, more hazard, more danger.

Nietzsche used to have a motto on his wall: LIVE DANGERously. Somebody asked him, "Why have you written this?" He said, "Just to remind me, because my fear is tremendous."

Live dangerously because that's the only way to live. There is no other. Always listen to the call of the unknown and be on the move. Never try to become settled anywhere. To be settled is to die; it is a premature death.

I was attending a small girl's birthday party, and many toys were there and many presents, and the girl was really happy, and all her friends were there and they were dancing. Suddenly, she asked her mother, "Mom, were there such beautiful days in the past, when you used to be alive?"

People die before their death. People settle in security, comfort, convenience. People settle into a gravelike existence.

I am not talking to your fear.

"Will existence really protect me if I allow myself to let go?" It has always protected, and I can't think it is going to be different just with you. I cannot believe that you are going to be an exception. It has always been so—existence has protected those who have left themselves to it, who have abandoned themselves to it, who have surrendered themselves to it.

Follow nature. Follow your inner nature.

I was reading an anecdote; I liked it very much:

> It was spring on the Columbia University campus, and KEEP
> OFF signs sprang up on the freshly seeded lawns. The students
> ignored the warnings, plus the special requests which followed,
> and continued tramping across the grass. The issue became
> rather heated, until finally the buildings and grounds officials

took the problem to Dwight Eisenhower, who was at that time
the president of the university.

"Did you ever notice," asked Eisenhower, "how much
quicker it is to head directly where you are going? Why not
find out which route the students are going to take anyway
and build the walks there?"

This is how life should be. The roads, the walks, the principles should not be fixed beforehand.

Allow yourself a let-go. Flow naturally and let that be your way. Walk, and by walking, make your way. Don't follow super-highways. They are dead, and you are not going to find anything on them. Everything has already been removed. If you follow a superhighway, you are moving away from nature. Nature knows no ways, no fixed patterns. It flows in a thousand and one patterns, but all spontaneous. Go and watch. Sit on the beach and watch the sea . . . millions of waves arising but each wave is unique and different. You cannot find two waves similar, they don't follow any pattern.

No human being worth the name will follow any pattern.

People come to me and they say, "Show us the way." I tell them, "Don't ask that. I can only show you how to walk—I cannot show you the way." Please try to see the distinction. I can only show you how to walk, and how to walk courageously. I cannot show you the way, because "the way" is for cowards. Those who don't know how to walk, paralyzed, for them the way exists. For those who know how to walk, they go into the wilderness, and just by walking they create their way.

And each one reaches the truth in a different way. You cannot reach as a mass and you cannot reach as a crowd. You reach alone, absolutely alone.

I teach you just to be yourself, nothing else. It is very difficult to understand me because out of your fear you would like me to give you a pattern of life, a discipline, a style, a way of life.

Persons like me have always been misunderstood. A Lao Tzu, a Zarathustra, an Epicurus, have always been misunderstood. The most religious people were thought to be irreligious because if someone is really religious he will teach you freedom, he will teach you love. He will not teach you law; he will teach you love. He will not teach you a dead pattern of life. He will teach you a chaos, an anarchy, because stars are born only out of chaos. He will teach you how to be totally free.

I know there is fear—there is fear of freedom; otherwise why should there be so many prisons all around the world? Why should people carry invisible prisons around their lives? There are only two types of prisoners—I have come across a few who live in a visible prison and the remaining who live in an invisible prison. They carry their prison around themselves—in the name of conscience, in the name of morality, in the name of tradition, in the name of this and that. Thousands are the names of bondage and slavery.

Freedom has no name. There are not many types of freedom; freedom is one. Have you ever watched? Truth is one. Lies can be millions. You can lie in a million ways; you cannot say the truth in a million ways. Truth is simple, one way is enough. Love is one; laws are millions. Freedom is one; prisons are many.

And unless you are very alert, you will never be able to move freely. At the most, you can change prisons. From one prison you can go to the other prison, and you can enjoy the walk between the two. That's what is happening in the world. A Catholic becomes a Communist, a Hindu becomes a Christian, a Mohammedan becomes a Hindu, and they enjoy, yes; there is a little freedom felt just when they are changing the prisons. From one prison to another, on the walk in between they feel good. Then they are in the same trap again, with a different name. All ideologies are prisons. I teach you to beware of them—my ideology included.

Move the Way Love Makes You Move

A line in a Rumi poem says, "Move within, but don't move the way fear makes you move." Sometimes in meditation I touch a blank horizontal space with no reference point for who I am, and a tremendous fear is there. Can you help me to understand and make friends with this fear?

The words of Mevlana Rumi are immensely significant. There have been very few people who have moved and transformed as many hearts as Jalaluddin Rumi has. In the world of the Sufis, Rumi is an emperor. His words have to be understood not as mere words, but sources of deep silences, echoes of inner and the innermost songs. More than twelve hundred years have passed since he was alive.

His technique for meditation is a special kind of dance. It is a kind of whirling, just the way small children whirl; standing on one spot they go on round and round. Everywhere in the world small children do that, and their elders stop them saying, "You will become dizzy, you will fall, you will hurt yourself," and, "What is the point of doing it?"

Jalaluddin Rumi made a meditation of whirling. The meditator goes on whirling for hours—as long as the body allows him; he does not stop on his own. When whirling, a moment comes that he sees himself utterly still and silent, a center of the cyclone. Around the center the body is moving, but there is a space which remains unmoved; that is his being.

Rumi himself whirled for thirty-six hours continuously and fell, because the body could not whirl anymore. But when he opened his eyes he was another man. Hundreds of people had gathered to see. Many had always thought he was mad: "What is the point of whirling? Nobody can say this is a prayer; nobody can say this is a great dance; nobody can say in any way that this has something to do with religion, spirituality." But after thirty-six hours when they saw Rumi so luminous, so radiant, so new, so fresh—reborn, in a new consciousness, they could not believe their eyes. Hundreds wept in repentance, because they had thought that he was mad. In fact he was sane and they were mad.

And down these twelve centuries the stream has continued to be alive. There are very few movements of spiritual growth that have lived so long continuously. There are still hundreds of dervishes. *Dervish* is the Sufi word for the spiritual seeker. You cannot believe it unless you experience, that just by whirling you can know yourself. No austerity is needed, no self-torture is needed, but just an experience of your innermost being and you are transported into another plane of existence from the mortal to the immortal. The darkness disappears and there is just eternal light.

Rumi's words have to be understood very carefully because he has not spoken much—just a few small poems. His statement, "Move within, but don't move the way fear makes you move"—it is so beautiful.

Don't move the way fear makes you move.

Move the way love makes you move. Move the way joy makes you move—not out of fear, because all so-called religions are based on fear. Their God is nothing but fear, and their heaven and hell are nothing but projections of fear and greed.

Rumi's statement is revolutionary: Do not move because of fear. All the religions say to people, "Fear God!" Mahatma Gandhi used to say, "I do not fear anybody but God." When I heard this I said this is the most stupid statement anybody can make. You can fear everybody, but don't fear God because God can only be approached through love. God is not a person but the universal heartbeat. If you can sing with love and dance with love—an ordinary activity like whirling with love—joy and celebration are enough to reach to the innermost sanctum of being and existence.

You all have been living out of fear. Your relationships are out of fear. Fear is so overwhelming, like a dark cloud covering your life, that you say things which you don't want to say, but fear makes you say them. You do things which you do not want to do, but fear makes you do them. A little intelligence is enough to see it.

Millions of people are worshipping stones carved by themselves. They have created their gods and then they worship them. It must be out of great fear, because in reality, where can you find God? The easier way is to carve a god in beautiful marble and worship it. And nobody thinks that this is sheer stupidity, because everybody else is also doing it, in different ways—somebody in the temple and somebody in the mosque and somebody in the synagogue; it does not make any difference. The essential thing is the same, that what you are doing is out of fear. Your prayers are full of fear.

Rumi is making a revolutionary, an extraordinary statement: "Move within, but don't move the way fear makes you move." Then what is the way to move within? Why not move playfully? Why not make your religion a playfulness? Why be so serious? Why not move laughingly? Just like small children running joyously after butterflies for no special reason, just the joy of the colors and the beauty of the flowers and the butterflies is enough—and they are so immensely happy.

In every twenty-four hours find a few moments that are fearless . . . which means in those moments you are not asking for anything. You are not asking for any reward and you are not worried about any punishment; you are simply enjoying the whirling, the going inward.

In fact, it is only in the beginning that it may look a little difficult. As you move a little inward you become automatically joyful, playful, prayerful. A gratitude arises in you that you have never known before and a space opens up which is infinite, your inner sky.

Your inner sky is not less rich than the outer sky: It has its own stars and its own moon and its own planets and its own immensity; it has exactly as vast a universe as you can see outside. You are just standing in between two universes—one is outside you; one is inside you. The outside universe consists of things, and the inside universe consists of consciousness, of bliss, of joy.

Move within, but don't move the way fear makes you move, because fear cannot enter inward.

Why can fear not enter inward? Fear cannot be alone, and inward you have to be alone. Fear needs a crowd, fear needs companionship, friends, even foes will do. But to be alone, to go inward, you cannot take anybody with you; you have to be more and more alone. Not only can you not take anyone, you cannot take any *thing* either. Your wealth, your power, your prestige—you cannot take anything. Inside you cannot take even your clothes! You will have to go nude and alone. Hence fear cannot move inward, fear moves outward.

Fear moves toward money, fear moves toward power, fear moves toward God; fear moves in all directions except inward.

To go inward the first requirement is fearlessness.

And you are wondering how to make friends with the fear. One has not to make friends with darkness, death, or fear. One has to get rid of them. One has to simply say good-bye forever. It is your attachment, and friendship will make it even more deep.

Don't think that by becoming friendly with fear you will become ready to go inward. Even the friendly fear will prevent it; in fact, it will prevent it more. It will prevent you in a friendly way, it will advise you, "Don't do such a thing. There is nothing inward. You will fall into a nothingness and returning from that nothingness is impossible. Beware of falling into your inwardness. Cling to things."

You don't have to make friends—fear has to be understood, and it disappears.

What are you afraid of? When you were born, you were born naked. You did not bring any bank balance either, but you were not afraid. You come into the world utterly nude, but entering like an emperor. Even an emperor cannot enter into the world the way a child enters. The same is true of entering inward. It is a second childbirth; you again become a child—the same innocence and the same nudity and the same nonpossessiveness. What do you have to be afraid of?

In life you cannot be afraid of birth. It has already happened, now nothing can be done about it. You cannot be afraid of life, it is already happening. You cannot be afraid of death—whatever you do it is going to happen. So what is the fear?

I have always been asked even by very learned people, "Do you never get concerned what will happen after death?" And I have always wondered at the fact that these people are considered learned. I have asked them, "One day I was not born, and there was no worry. I have never for a single moment thought about what kind of trouble, what kind of anxiety, what kind of anguish I had to face when I was not yet born. I was simply not! So the same will be the case—when you die, you die."

Confucius was asked by his most significant disciple, Mencius, "What will happen after death?"

Confucius said, "Don't waste time. When you are in your grave, lie down and think over it, but why bother now?"

Fear of what will happen when you die is unnecessary. Whatever will happen will happen—and anyway you cannot do anything about it beforehand. You don't know, so there is no question of doing some homework, getting ready for the kind of questions you will be asked, or what kind of people you will meet, learning their customs, their language . . . We don't know anything; there is no need to worry. Don't waste time.

But it is fear, fear that something is going to happen. After death—and you will be so alone; even if you call from your grave nobody is going to hear you.

I have heard about a phenomenon in America called "The

Couch Potato Movement." It was created for people who sit at home all day and watch TV. It was started in 1982, and became a great phenomenon. Two books were published, *The Official Couch Potato Handbook* and *The Couch Potato Guide to Life*. It also had a newsletter, "The Tuber's Voice." The founder of the movement was spreading the Couch Potato gospel: "We feel that watching TV is an indigenous American form of meditation." He said, "We call it Transcendental Vegetation."

Out of fear people can do anything. They can even become a member of the Couch Potato Movement! Just sitting for seven, eight hours per day like a potato on the sofa, and growing fatter and fatter and fatter. . . . Once in a while they get up to go to the fridge; otherwise, they are doing their Transcendental Vegetation. It has never been done on such a vast scale.

Why should people watch television the whole day? One has to look into the psychology. These people simply don't want to know anything about themselves. These people are trying to avoid themselves by watching television. Television is a substitute; otherwise, having so much time you will have to look inward—and that is a fear.

Inward? But the fridge is outward. Inward? But the boyfriend is outward. Inward you will not find anything. You cannot go shopping. You will just get drowned in nothingness. This being drowned in nothingness creates fear.

But the problem is that this fear arises only because you don't know the beauty and the bliss and the joy of drowning in nothingness, because you don't know the ecstasy that opens up as you fall inward. It needs a little taste.

I don't want you to believe, I want you to experiment.

If thousands of mystics have experienced something inside, at least hypothetically, you can also have a look. Perhaps there may be something that you are missing.

There is no question of fear, just a little intelligence is needed— not friendliness with fear but an intelligence—the adventurer's heart, the courage of those who go into the unknown. They are the blessed ones, because they find the meaning and the significance of life. Others only vegetate.

A little intelligence, a little sense of humor, a loving heart, and you don't need much else to enter into your own being. Serious people go on standing outside with long English faces.

Father Murphy wants to raise money for his church and he has heard that there is a fortune to be made in horse racing. However, he does not have enough money to buy a horse, so he decides to buy a donkey instead and enters him in a race. To his surprise the donkey comes in third. The headline on the sports page reads: "Priest's Ass Shows."

Father Murphy enters it in another race and this time it wins. The headline reads: "Priest's Ass Out Front."

The bishop is so upset by this kind of publicity that he orders Father Murphy not to race his donkey again. The headline reads: "Bishop Scratches Priest's Ass."

This is too much for the bishop. So he orders Father Murphy to get rid of the donkey. He gives it to Sister Theresa. And the headline reads: "Nun Has Best Ass in Town."

The bishop faints. He then informs Sister Theresa that she must dispose of the donkey. She sells it to Paddy for ten dollars.

The next day the bishop is found dead on the dining room table with a newspaper clutched in his hand. The headline reads: "Nun Sells Her Ass for Ten Bucks."

Just a little sense of humor, a little laughter, a childlike innocence—and what have you got to lose? What is the fear? We don't have anything. We have come without anything, we will go without anything. Before it happens, just a little adventure inward to see who is this fellow hiding behind the clothes, inside the skeleton; who is this person who is born, becomes a youth, falls in love and one day dies and nobody knows where he goes. . . .

Just a little curiosity to inquire into one's own being. It is very natural; there is no question of fear.

Drowning in Nothingness

Can you talk a little more about this phenomenon you call "drowning in nothingness"? To me it seems more like falling into empty space, and makes me feel very insecure and shaky.

The English word *empty* comes from a root which means at leisure, unoccupied. It is a beautiful word if you go to the root. The root is very pregnant; it means at leisure, unoccupied. Whenever you are unoccupied, at leisure, you are empty.

And remember, the proverb that says that the empty mind is the devil's workshop is just nonsense. Just the opposite is the truth—the occupied mind is the devil's workshop. The empty mind is God's workshop, not the devil's. But you have to understand what I mean by "empty"—at leisure, relaxed, not tense, not moving, not desiring, not going anywhere. Just being here, utterly here. An empty mind is a pure presence. And all is possible in that pure presence, because the whole existence comes out of that pure presence.

These trees grow out of that pure presence, these stars are born out of this pure presence; we are here—all the buddhas have come out of this pure presence. In that pure presence you are in God, you *are* God. Occupied, you fall; occupied, you have to be expelled from the Garden of Eden. Unoccupied you are back in the garden, unoccupied you are back at home.

When the mind is not occupied by reality—by things, by thoughts—then there is that which is. And that which is, is the truth. Only in emptiness is there a meeting, merging. Only in emptiness do you open to truth and truth enters in you. Only in emptiness do you become pregnant with truth.

These are the three states of the mind. The first is consciousness plus content. You always have contents in the mind—a thought moving, a desire arising, anger, greed, ambition. You always have some content in the mind; the mind is never unoccupied. The traffic goes on, day in, day out. While awake it is there, while asleep it is there. While awake you call it thinking, while asleep you call it dreaming—it is the same process. Dreaming is a little more primitive, that's all—because it thinks in pictures. It does not use concepts, it uses pictures. It is more primitive; like small children think in pictures. So in small children's books you have to make big pictures, colorful, because they think through pictures. Through pictures they will learn words. By and by those pictures become smaller and smaller, and then they disappear.

The primitive man also thinks in pictures, and the most ancient languages are pictorial. Chinese, for example, is a pictorial language; it has no alphabet.

In the night you again become primitive, you forget the sophistication of your day and you start thinking in pictures—but it is the same. And the psychoanalyst's insight is valuable—he looks into your dreams. Then there is more truth, because you are more primitive; you are not trying to deceive anybody, you are more authentic.

In the day you have a personality around you that hides you—layers upon layers of personality. It is very difficult to find the true person; you will have to dig deep, and it hurts, and the person will resist. But in the night, just as you put your clothes away, you put your personality away too. It is not needed because you will not be communicating with anybody, you will be alone in your bed. You will not be in the world, you will be absolutely in your private realm, so there is no need to hide and no need to pretend. That's why the psychoanalyst tries to go into your dreams, because they show much more clearly who you are.

But it is the same game played in different languages; the game is not different. This is the ordinary state of the mind—mind and content, consciousness plus content.

The second state of the mind is consciousness *without* content; that's what meditation is. You are fully alert, and there is a gap, an interval. No thought is encountered, there is no thought within you. You are not asleep, you are awake—but there is no thought. This is meditation. The first state is called mind, the second state is called meditation.

And then there is a third state. When the content has disappeared, the object has disappeared, the subject cannot remain for long because they exist together. They produce each other. When the subject is alone, it can only hang around a little while longer just out of its past momentum. Without the content, the consciousness cannot be there long; it will not be needed, because a consciousness is always a consciousness *of* something. When you say you are "conscious," it can be asked, "Of what?" You say, "I am conscious *of*. . ." That object is needed, it is a must for the subject to exist. Once the object has disappeared, soon the subject will also disappear. First the contents go, then consciousness disappears.

This third state is called *samadhi*—no content, no consciousness. But remember, this no-content, no-consciousness, is not a state of *unconsciousness*. It is a state of superconsciousness, of transcendental consciousness. Consciousness now is only conscious of itself. Consciousness has turned upon itself; the circle is complete. You have come home. This is the third state, *samadhi*; and this third state is what Buddha means by *shunyata*, emptiness.

First drop the content—you become half-empty, then drop consciousness—you become fully empty. And this full-emptiness is the most beautiful thing that can happen, the greatest benediction.

In this nothingness, in this emptiness, in this selflessness, in this *shunyata*, there is complete security and stability.

You will be surprised to know this—complete security and stability when you are *not*? All fears disappear . . . because what is the basic fear? The basic fear is the fear of death. All other fears are just reflections of the basic fear. All other fears can be reduced to one fear: The fear of death, the fear that, "One day I may have to disappear, one day I may have to die. I am, and the day is coming when I will not be"—that frightens, that is the fear.

To avoid that fear we start moving in such a way so that we can live as long as possible. And we try to secure our lives—we start compromising, we start becoming more and more secure, safe, because of the fear. We become paralyzed, because the more secure you are, the more "safe" you are, the less alive you will be.

Life exists in challenges, life exists in crises, life needs insecurity. It grows in the soil of insecurity. Whenever you are insecure, you will find yourself more alive, more alert. That's why so many rich people become dull: A kind of stupidity and a kind of stupor surrounds them. They are so secure, there is no challenge. They are so secure, they need not be intelligent. They are so secure—for what do they need intelligence? Intelligence is needed when there is challenge, intelligence is provoked by challenge.

So because of the fear of death we strive for security, for a bank balance, for insurance, for marriage, for a settled life, for a home. We become part of a country, we join a political party, we join a church—we become Hindus, Christians, Mohammedans. These are all ways to find security. These are all ways to find someplace to belong to—a country, a church.

And because of this fear politicians and priests go on exploiting you. If you are not in any fear, no politician, no priest can exploit you. It is only out of fear that they can exploit because they can provide—at least they can promise—that what they have will make you secure: "This will be your security. I can guarantee it." The goods may never be delivered, that's another thing, but the promise is there, and the promise keeps people exploited and oppressed. The promise keeps people in bondage.

Once you have known this inner emptiness then there is no fear, because death has already happened. In that emptiness it has happened. In that emptiness you have disappeared, how can you be afraid anymore? About what? About whom? And who can be afraid? In this emptiness all fear disappears because death has already happened. Now there is no longer any death possible. You feel a kind of deathlessness, timelessness. Eternity has arrived. Now you don't look for security; there is no need.

This is the state of a sannyasin; this is the state where you need not be a part of a country, need not be a part of a church, or stupid things like that.

It is only when you have become nothing that you can be yourself. It looks paradoxical . . .

You need not compromise, because it is out of fear and greed that one compromises. And you can live in rebellion because there is nothing to lose. You can *become* a rebellion; there is nothing to fear. Nobody can kill you, you have already done that thing yourself. Nobody can take anything away from you; you have dropped all that which can be taken away from you. Now you are in nothingness. You are a nothingness; hence the paradoxical phenomenon that in this nothingness arises a great security, a great safety, a stability because there is no more death possible.

And with death, time disappears. With death disappear all the problems that are created by death and by time. In the wake of all these disappearances, what is left is a pure sky. This pure sky is *samadhi*, nirvana.

The Prison of "I"

Hamlet's ultimate question is, "To be or not to be?" My ultimate question to you is, "To be and not to be?" How is it possible?

Shakespeare is a great poet, but not a mystic. He has an intuition into the reality of things, but it is only a glimpse, very vague, as if seen in a dream, not clear. His question in *Hamlet* shows that unclarity. "To be or not to be?" can never be asked by a man who knows, because there is no question of choice. You cannot choose between "to be" or "not to be."

In existential terms, not to be is the only way to be. Unless you disappear you are not really there. It looks a little difficult to understand, because basically it is irrational. But reason is not the way of existence; existence is as irrational as you can conceive.

Here, those who think they are, are not. And those who think and realize that they are not—only they are.

The idea that "I am" is just an idea, a projection of the mind. But the realization that "I am not" comes only as a flowering of meditation. When you realize, "I am not," only the "I" disappears and there remains behind a pure existence, undefined, unbounded, unfettered, just a pure space.

"I" is a great prison. It is your slavery and bondage to the mind.

The moment you enter beyond the mind, you *are*—but you don't have any notion of being an ego, of being an "I". In other words: The more you think you are, the less you are; the more you experience that you are not . . . the more you are. The moment the soap bubble of your ego pops, you have become the whole existence.

Yes, something has disappeared . . . before you were just a dewdrop, now you are the whole ocean! You are not a loser. You were encaged in a very small, limited space, and that imprisonment is our misery, our pain, our anguish. From every side we are enclosed, on every side we encounter a thick wall—we cannot move.

Have you ever experienced in a nightmare, in a dream . . . you know perfectly well that your eyes are open, and you want to move your hands but you cannot; you want to get up, but you cannot. A tremendous fear grips you as if you are paralyzed for the moment. That experience will explain to you our whole life as a dewdrop. Our intrinsic nature is to be oceanic, and to force an ocean into a dewdrop is certain to create anxiety, anguish, misery, agony.

Shakespeare's question, "To be or not to be?" is only intellectual—and it is bound to be intellectual, because he was not a man of realization. He was very talented, there have been only a few poets of his caliber. But to be a poet is one thing—and to know existence from inside, not from outside, is another.

The poet looks at the beauty of the flower, at the beauty of the sunset, at the beauty of the starry night, but he is always on the outside, an observer, a spectator; he is never an insider. That is the difference between a poet and a mystic. When the poet sees the rose, the rose is there outside the poet, and the poet is there outside the rose.

When the mystic sees the rose, he is the rose.

All differences, all distinctions, all distances have disappeared.

In such moments the seers of the Upanishads have declared: *Aham brahmasmi*—I am God. It is not a declaration of ego; it is simply a declaration of the mystical experience of being one with the ultimate reality. But it is true on smaller scales too.

The mystic can say, "I am the rose, I am the stars, I am the ocean." The poet cannot say that. He can say that the rose is beautiful, he can make an observation and a judgment about the rose, but he cannot melt and merge into the reality of the rose. He cannot get lost into it, he cannot become one with it, he cannot drop the duality. However great his insight as a poet may be, it will remain based in duality. Certainly the poet sees more beauty than you see. He has clearer eyes, he has a more loving heart and he has a different approach than the scientist.

The scientist looks at the rose flower from the intellect, from the mind. The poet looks from the heart, from intuition. He is certainly deeper than the scientist. The scientist in fact cannot see the beauty of the rose; all he can do is try to dissect the rose to find out where the beauty is. And the moment the rose is dissected, all beauty disappears . . . hence for the scientist there is no beauty, because the beauty cannot survive the dissection. Hence for the scientist there is no life, because the moment you dissect a living being what you find are dead parts, you never find life.

The mystic is just the very opposite of the scientist. The scientist tries to know things by dissecting them, and the mystic tries to know things by dropping the distance, the gap between himself and reality. His approach is of the being. These are the three approaches. The approach of the mind—that is what the scientist is doing. The approach of the heart—that is what the poet, the painter, the artist is doing. And the approach of the being—that is the world of the mystic.

Shakespeare is great in his poetic compositions, his intuition is deep. But he is not a mystic; otherwise he could not have made the statement, "To be or not to be?"

There is no choice; they are not two.

The only way to be is not to be.

Disappear if you want real existence, authentic existence; merge into reality, dissolve your ice cube in the ocean and become one with it. Of course you will get lost as a separate entity, but you will become the whole. It is not a loss; it is a tremendous gain.

You are asking, "My ultimate question to you is: To be *and* not to be?" That is not a question; that is the only way you can find yourself. But first comes "not to be," and second comes "to be." That is the only change I would like to make in your question. You say, "To be and not to be?"—"not to be" has to be first, then "to be" follows. You have just to give space. Throw out all the furniture that is filling your space. And the greatest block is the ego— throw it out!

Let the temple of your being be utterly empty. That is the state of "not to be."

And you will be surprised . . . here you are trying "not to be," and from the back door comes a new realization of being, of "to be." But your effort should not be based in this order—first to be and then not to be. That is against the natural process of enlightenment. You have to attain nothingness first, nobodiness first. This is the price you have to pay for attaining to the experience of authentic being. This is the sacrifice you have to make. This is what Jesus means when he says, "Unless you are born again, you will not enter into the kingdom of God." What does he mean when he says, "Unless you are born again"? He means first you have to die, and after death is resurrection.

As the ego dies it allows space for your authentic being to blossom. On the grave of your ego blossoms the lotus of your being. But remember, you have to change your statement because in this statement your ego lingers. "To be" is your first desire. But if that is your first desire, then it will be very difficult, almost impossible, to allow "not to be." You will cling to your ego.

You are saying, "To be and not to be." One thing is certainly right, that both have to exist together . . . but which is to be the first? You cannot start from the wrong end. You have to start by being nobody, by simply being spacious. In that spaciousness the guest arrives.

But it is natural . . . the way you have put your question is natural to the mind.

It happened: A man came to Gautam Buddha with almost the same question that you have raised here. Gautam Buddha said to him, "First you have to drop your ego and then you need not worry; everything happens of its own accord, spontaneously."

The man said, "If that is the way to realize myself, then I will make every effort to drop the ego."

Buddha said, "You have not understood me. You are still trying to realize yourself. You are even ready to drop the ego, but the desire deep down is to find a truer ego, a more eternal ego; that's what you are calling the self. Forget about the self. There is nothing to be achieved! You have simply to drop your ego and wait."

There is no question of any effort to be made; no achievement is going to be there. What happens, happens of its own accord. You cannot claim that it is your realization. That's why Gautam Buddha is the first person in the history of man who has not used the expression "self-realization." He came to know that so many people, under the disguise of the word *self*, are simply protecting their ego. They are calling it self-realization, but they really mean ego-realization. They have a disguised desire to make their ego permanent and eternal.

Seeing this cunningness of the human mind, Buddha simply dropped the words self and self-realization. He stopped talking about what will happen when your ego is dropped. He said, "That is not my business and that is not your business either. You simply drop the ego and wait and see what happens, but don't conceive it from the very beginning. Don't make it a goal, an ambition. The moment you make it an ambition, the ego has come back from the hidden, secret door of your being."

Buddha was very much misunderstood. It was obvious, particularly in India where for thousands of years before him the religious people had been talking about self-realization. But Gautam Buddha had a far deeper and clearer insight than anyone who preceded him. He saw behind this idea of self-realization nothing but a deep ego.

He changed the whole language of spirituality. In the language he used to speak—Pali is its name—the self is called *atta*. Buddha dropped the word completely and he started using a negative word, *anatta*. *Atta* means self; *anatta* means no-self. It was against the whole tradition, not only of this country but of all the countries. Nobody had ever heard about no-self, no-mind, no-realization.

Then people started asking him, "What is the point of all this effort, meditation, disciplines, fasting, austerities . . . ? What is the point if finally we are going to be nobody? It is a strange effort! Such a long journey, so arduous, just to find in the end that you are not."

What they were saying was logical. But whenever you

encounter a man like Gautam Buddha, his love is far stronger than your logic can ever be. His presence is far stronger than your reason, your mind, your personality, your ambitions, your desires. His very presence is so powerful, so magnetic that people start—against themselves, in spite of themselves—on a journey which ends in no-self.

A man like Gautam Buddha has a certain magnetic attraction, very subtle. Things don't move toward him but souls move, consciousnesses move, life forces move. It is his presence that gives you the proof that not-being is not death, not-being is the ultimate in life.

But remember, not-being is the first thing; that is your meditation, that is your death. Out of this meditation, out of this death, out of this nothingness will arise your original face, your original being. So you will have to change just a little bit. Put not-being first. That has to be the priority. You need not be concerned about being, it comes. It comes absolutely without any exception.

I am saying it based on my own experience too. I had to disappear into nothingness—and out of that nothingness a totally new, utterly fresh, eternal presence has arisen. It is not my doing. I cannot take any credit for it. At the most I allowed it to happen, because I was not there to disturb. Your not-being is necessary first so that you don't disturb when your being starts arising . . . just a little change.

Old Hymie Goldberg returned to the doctor to express his delight over the invisible hearing aid that his doctor had fitted for him.

"I bet your family likes it too," said the doctor.

"Ah no," said old Hymie, "they don't know about it yet and I am having a great time. In the past two days, I have changed my will twice!"

You also have to change your will. What you have put as secondary has to be primary, and what you have put as primary is not your concern. It will come, just as when spring comes, flowers come on their own accord.

4

MAKE LOVE, NOT FEAR—
TRUSTING ONESELF
AND OTHERS

Everybody's life, more or less, is governed by fear, because there are only two ways to live life. Either it can be governed by love, or it can be governed by fear. Ordinarily, unless you have learned to love, it is governed by fear.

Without love, fear is bound to be there. It is just an absence of love. It has nothing positive in it; it is just absence of love. But if you can love, fear disappears. In the moment of love there is not even death.

There is only one thing in life that conquers death and that is love. All fear is concerned with death—and only love can conquer death.

So one thing I would like to say to you is, don't pay too much attention to fear because it becomes an autohypnosis. If you go on repeating that you live in fear, that your life is governed by fear, you are dominated by fear, then you are helping it. Take note of it: that your life is governed by fear—finished! It simply shows that love has not yet become so powerful that fear disappears.

Fear is just a symptom, it is not a disease. There is no cure for it; there is no need. So it is just a symptom, and it is very useful because it shows you that you should not waste your life any longer. It simply says to you to love more.

So I will not talk about fear. I will help you to love more—and fear disappears as a consequence. If you start working directly on fear you strengthen it, because your whole attention will be focused on it. It is as if somebody is trying to destroy darkness, and becomes focused, obsessed, with how to destroy darkness. You cannot destroy darkness because it is not there in the first place. Note the fact that darkness is there—and then start working on how to bring in light.

The same energy that you are using to fight fear can be used to love. Pay more attention to love. If you touch, touch as lovingly as possible; as if your hand becomes your whole being and you are flowing through your hand. You will feel energy passing through it, a certain warmth, a glow. If you make love, go wild and forget all civilization. Forget all that has been taught about love; just be wild and love like animals.

Once you realize that the presence of love becomes the absence of fear, you have got the point and there is no problem.

. . .

When man lives in fear, he becomes hard. It is fear that creates hardness. In fear we close up; we close all doors and all windows. We start living in a very small, dark hole. Our life already becomes death. And we create an armor around ourselves, a hard, steel armor, so that we are protected and safe and secure.

This is not a way to live life; this is a way to commit suicide. This is real suicide. This is already entering into your grave, because this type of closed existence will not be able to know anything of truth, of beauty, of love, of bliss, of godliness. If nothing is allowed in, how can you know what surrounds you? And if you don't know what surrounds you, you will never be able to know yourself. One can know oneself only in reference to the other. First you have to know the "thou," then you can know "I."

Psychologists say the child first becomes aware of the others: the mother, the father, the brothers, sisters, the family, the things that surround him, the room, the walls, the toys. Then slowly he comes closer and closer . . . then he becomes aware of his body. And then one day he starts feeling himself as a separate individual. First he becomes aware of the other, and then in reference to the other he becomes defined. The other gives the definition.

A person who lives in possessions will not know his real self, because he lives surrounded in things, and things can only define you as a thing; they cannot define you as a soul.

Only in deep love does one become aware of one's soul, because in deep love one becomes aware of the other's soul, and the other's soul creates a response in you, creates a resonance in you. Suddenly you are aware of a new dimension, of something that is beyond time and space. The "thou" becomes the mirror to know one's own face. Love is the best mirror to show you who you are.

The closed person never knows who he is, he cannot know. And all that he knows about himself is false; he lives with a false identity. He thinks he is his name and his money and his power and his prestige, and that is all nonsense—he is none of those things. He is something divine, something that exists before birth and that will exist after death . . . but he will not be aware of it.

One has to become soft, vulnerable, open. One has to become almost like a sponge, so that the sun and the rain and the wind are all allowed, invited, accepted, welcomed, so that existence can penetrate you. And one has to allow existence to reach to one's deepest core, because that is the only way—if existence goes deep into your being—that you will become aware of your depths. If it penetrates to the very core, you will become aware of your center. And that's what is meant by self-knowledge.

But one has to learn how to be soft, how to drop all armor, how to open the doors and windows, how not to cling anymore to fear—how to be in love with the trees and the mountains and the rivers and the people . . . because love is the key that unlocks your doors. You open to somebody only when you are in love, because then you are no longer afraid. You can allow the other to reach you, you can trust. You know the other will not hurt you.

The day one trusts the whole of existence, the day one knows, "It is not going to hurt me because I am part of it—how can the whole hurt the part? Because my pain will be its pain, my misery is going to be its misery . . ." When you are miserable, a part of existence is miserable. When you are crying, existence is crying because your tears are the tears of the whole. All eyes are the eyes of the whole, and all hands are the hands of existence. The whole, the divine, has no other eyes and no other hands. So when your eyes are full of tears and your heart full of pain, existence is full of pain and full of tears. How can the whole hurt or wound the part? It is impossible! It is an unnecessary fear.

The only thing that I teach is to drop fear. It is absolutely un-necessary, and it is crippling you, paralyzing you. It is a slow kind of poison that kills people, destroys people. They live and yet they live not, they only die. They die over a long period of time, seventy years, eighty years, slowly, part by part. They don't commit suicide in a single moment, hence it is not known as suicide—but it is sui-cide.

My observation is that 99 percent of people commit suicide. It is a very rare person who lives, who really lives. That person has to be courageous enough to be open to all kinds of experiences, to be open unconditionally.

The Fear of Intimacy

Why do I feel fear when somebody comes close to me? Is it just a lack of trust?

Trust is possible only if first you trust in yourself. The most fundamental thing has to happen within you first. If you trust in yourself you can trust in people, you can trust in existence. But if you don't trust in yourself then no other trust is ever possible.

And everybody feels fear, more or less. That's why people don't allow others to come very close; that's why people avoid love. Sometimes in the very name of love they go on avoiding love. People keep each other at a distance—they allow the other only so far, then the fear arises.

What is the fear? The fear is that the other may be able to see your emptiness if they come too close. It has nothing to do with the other—you have never been able to accept your inner empti-ness, that's the fear. You have created a very, very decorated sur-face. You have a beautiful face and you have a good smile and you talk well and you are very articulate and you sing well and you have a beautiful body and a beautiful persona. But those are on the surface. Behind them is simple emptiness. You are afraid that if somebody comes too close they will be able to see past the mask, past your smile, they will be able to see beneath your words. That frightens you. You know that there is nothing else, you are just a surface—that is the fear—you don't have any depth.

It is not that you *cannot* have the depth—you can have it, but you have not taken the first step. The first step is to accept this inner emptiness with joy, and to go into it. Don't avoid your inner emptiness. If you avoid your inner emptiness you will avoid people coming closer to you. If you rejoice in your emptiness you will be completely open and you will invite people to come close to you and to have a look into your innermost shrine. Because when it is accepted, the emptiness has a certain quality, but when it is rejected it has a different quality.

The difference is in your mind. If you reject it, it looks like death; if you accept it, the same thing becomes the very source of life.

Only through meditation will you be able to allow others to come close to you. Only through meditation, when you have started feeling your inner emptiness as joy, as celebration, as song, when your inner emptiness no longer freaks you out, when your inner emptiness no longer frightens you, when your inner emptiness is a solace, a shelter, a refuge, a rest—and whenever you are tired you simply drown into your inner emptiness, you disappear there—when you have started loving your inner emptiness and the joy that arises out of it, thousands of lotuses flower in that emptiness. They float in the lake of emptiness.

But you are so afraid of being empty that you don't look at it. You make every effort to avoid it. You will listen to the radio, you will go to the movie, you will look at the TV, you will read the newspaper, the detective story—something, anything, but you will be continuously avoiding your inner emptiness. When tired you will fall asleep and you will dream, but you never face it. You never hold it close to you, you never hug it. That's the reason.

You ask, "Why do I feel fear when somebody comes close to me?" It is a great insight that has happened to you. Everybody feels fear when somebody comes close, but very few people are aware of it. People allow closeness only conditionally—the woman is your wife, then you allow her to sleep in your bed, to be with you in the night. But still you keep an invisible wall between you and the wife. The wall is invisible, but it is there. If you want to see it, observe it, you can find it—a transparent wall, a glass wall, but it is there. You remain private to yourself, your wife remains private to herself. Your privacies never meet. You have your secrets, she has her secrets. You are not really open and available to each other.

Even in love you don't allow the other to really come into you, you don't allow the other to penetrate you. And remember, if you allow the other to penetrate you there is great bliss. When two lovers' bodies penetrate each other there is a physical orgasm, when two minds penetrate each other there is a psychological orgasm, and when two spirits penetrate each other there is a spiritual orgasm.

You may not even have heard about the other two. Even the first is a rarity. Very few people attain to the real physical orgasm, they have forgotten about it. They think that ejaculation is orgasm. So many men believe that they have orgasm—and because women don't ejaculate, at least not visibly, 80 percent of women think they don't have any orgasm. But ejaculation is not orgasm. It is just a local release, a sexual release—it is not orgasm. A release is a negative phenomenon—you simply lose energy—and orgasm is a totally different thing. It is a dance of energy, not a release. It is an ecstatic state of energy. The energy becomes a flow. And it is all over the body; it is not sexual, it is physical. Each cell and each fiber of your body throbs with new joy. It is rejuvenated . . . and great peace follows it.

But people don't even know physical orgasm, so what to say about, how to talk about the psychological orgasm? When you allow somebody to come very close to you—a friend, a beloved, a son, a father, it does not matter what kind of relationship—when you allow somebody so close that your minds start overlapping, penetrating, then there is something so beyond the physical orgasm that it is a jump. The physical orgasm was beautiful, but nothing compared to the psychological orgasm. Once you have known the psychological orgasm, physical orgasm by and by loses its attraction. It is a very poor substitute.

But even the psychological orgasm is nothing compared to the spiritual orgasm, when two spirits—and by "spirits" I mean two emptinesses, two zeros—overlap. Remember, two bodies can only touch; they cannot overlap because they are physical. How can two bodies be in the same space? It is impossible. So at the most you can have a close touch. Two bodies can only touch; even in sexual love two bodies only touch. The penetration is very superficial, it is not more than a touch, because two physical objects cannot exist in the same place. If I am sitting here in this chair then nobody else can sit in the same place. If a stone is lying in a certain place, you cannot put another thing in the same place. The space is occupied.

Physical objects occupy space, so two physical objects can only touch—and that is part of the misery of love. If you know only physical love you will always be miserable because you will only be touching, and the deep desire is to become one. But two physical objects cannot become one. It is not possible.

A better communion happens with two psyches. They can come closer. But even then, two thoughts cannot occupy the same space because thoughts are subtle things. They can touch far better, they can become intertwined far better than two things . . . things are very solid, thoughts are very liquid. When two lovers' bodies meet it is like two stones coming together; when two psyches meet, it is like water and oil coming together. Yes, it is a better meeting but still there is a subtle division. Two thoughts cannot occupy the same space. When you are thinking one thought, you cannot think another thought at the same time—the first thought will have to go, only then will you be able to pay attention to another thought. Only one thought can be in your mind at one time and in one space. So even friendship, psychological friendship, misses something, lacks something. It is better than the first but nothing compared with the third.

Spiritual penetration is the only possibility of really being one with someone—because spirit means emptiness. Two emptinesses can be together. And not only two, all the emptiness of the world can be together in one space. They can occupy the same space simultaneously, at the same time, there is no problem—because they are neither concrete like objects nor liquid like water. They are simply empty of themselves. You can bring an infinite number of emptinesses together.

When you start feeling your emptiness—joyously, remember—

then you will be able to allow people to come close to you. Not only will you be able to allow them, you will be always welcoming, inviting—because whenever somebody can come into you, the only way is if he also allows you to come into him. There is no other way. If you want to come into me, the only way is to allow me to come into you. There is no other way.

But as you are, whenever something starts happening you become afraid, you start escaping.

Remember it—when something is very frightening remember that this is the time not to go anywhere, this is the time to be *here*. When something frightening is happening, then *something is happening*. The moment is very pregnant and you have to be here, and you have to go into it.

This is a good insight—that you ask why you feel fear whenever somebody comes close. You are becoming a little bit aware of your emptiness. Now let this awareness increase; let this awareness become a great experience. Go into this emptiness and soon you will be surprised that this emptiness is what meditation is, this emptiness is what I call divinity, godliness. And then you will become a temple—open to every stranger who wants to come in.

Afraid of Yourself

If I look at my own situation, I see that I'm so afraid of other people that the question of allowing them to come close doesn't even arise! What is this fear of others?

If you are afraid of yourself, only then are you afraid of other people. If you love yourself, you love others. If you hate yourself, you hate others. In relationship with others, it is only you—mirrored. The other is nothing but a mirror. So whatsoever happens in relationship, always know that it must have happened before, within you—because the relationship can only magnify what is already within you. It cannot create; it can only show and manifest what is already there.

If you love yourself, you love others. If you are afraid of yourself, you are afraid of others. In coming in contact with others you will start manifesting your being.

You have been conditioned—in the East, in the West, everywhere, Christian, Hindu, Mohammedan, Jain—you all have been conditioned to hate yourselves. It has been taught to you that to love yourself is bad. You are supposed to love others, not yourself. This is asking for absurdities, impossibilities—if you don't love yourself, and you are nearest to you, how can you love anybody else? Nobody loves himself yet he is trying to love others. Then your love is nothing but hatred masked, hidden.

I tell you to love yourself first, because if love happens within you, only then can it spread to others. It is just like throwing a stone into a silent lake. The stone falls, ripples arise, and then they go on moving, moving to the farthest bank. They will go on and on and on, but the stone must have fallen within you first.

Love has to have happened to you. You must love yourself; that is a basic requirement—which is missing all over the world. That's why the world is in such misery. Everybody is trying to love but it is impossible to love because the base is not there, the foundation is lacking.

Love yourself, and then suddenly you will find yourself reflected everywhere.

You are a human being and all other human beings are just like you. Just forms differ, names differ, but the reality is the same. Go

on moving, farther and farther; then animals are also like you—
the form differs a little more. But the being? Then the trees are
also like you. Go farther and farther, the ripples spread; then even
rocks, because they also exist like you. Existence is the same,
similar.

This is the only way: Start by loving yourself and let the love
spread. Then don't let there be any boundaries; go on and on to
the very infinity.

But if you miss the first point, if the stone has not been thrown
then you can go on waiting and watching but the ripples will
never arise. . . . It cannot start anywhere else; it can only start in
your heart. Love is a ripple in the heart, a vibration in the heart, a
throbbing, a sharing of whatsoever you are, a deep, intense urge to
go and reach the other, to share your being and your delight and
your song. But when your heart is almost dead, frozen, and you
have been taught to condemn yourself—that you are ugly, that
you are bad, that this is sin, "don't do this, you are guilty"—then
you cannot accept yourself. How can you accept anybody else?

A deep acceptance is needed. Whatsoever and whosoever you
are, a deep acceptance is needed—not only acceptance but a delight that you *are*. There should not be any "ought." Drop all
"shoulds" and the whole world becomes different. Right now, you
continuously think, "I should be this and that; then I can love and
be loved."

Even your God is nothing but the greatest condemner looking
at you from the skies, saying, "Behave!" This gives you a bad feeling about yourself. By and by, you become afraid because you are
suppressing yourself. If you relate with somebody, the suppression
may break and everything may bubble up to the surface. Then

what? So you are afraid, afraid to come in contact with anything and you remain hidden within yourself. Nobody knows how ugly you are, nobody knows how angry you are. Nobody knows how full of hatred you are, nobody knows your jealousy, possessiveness, envy. Nobody knows. You create armor around yourself and you live within that armor. So that you can manage your image, you never make any contact. If you come into contact with another person deeply, the image is bound to break. The reality, the real encounter will shatter it—that is the fear.

You ask, "Why am I afraid of other people?" You are afraid because you are afraid of yourself.

Drop that fear. Drop the guilt that has been created in you. Your politicians, priests, parents, all are guilt-creators because that is the only way that you can be controlled and manipulated. It is a very simple but very cunning trick to manipulate you. They have condemned you because if you are accepted, not condemned—if you are loved, appreciated, and if it is relayed to you from every-where that you are okay—then it will be difficult to control you.

How to control a person who is absolutely okay? The very problem doesn't arise. So they go on saying—the priests, the politicians, the parents—that you are not okay. Once they create the feeling that you are not okay, now they have become dicta-tors; now they have to dictate the discipline: "This is the way you should behave." First they create the feeling that you are wrong; then they give you guidelines for how to be right.

Accept yourself as you are, because that is the only way you can be. That's how the whole has willed you to be. That is what the whole has destined it to be. Relax, and accept, and delight— and there is transformation. It comes not by effort; it comes by accepting yourself with such deep love and ecstasy that there is no condition, conscious or unconscious, known or unknown. Unconditional acceptance—and suddenly you see you are not afraid of people. Rather, you enjoy people. People are beautiful. They are all manifestations of godliness. You love them, and if you love them you bring their godliness to the surface.

Whenever you love a person that person's godliness comes to the top. It happens—because when somebody loves you, how can you show your ugliness? Simply, your beautiful face comes up. By and by, the ugly face disappears. Love is alchemical. If you love yourself, the ugly part of you disappears, is absorbed, is transformed. The energy is released from that form.

Everything carries energy. Your anger has much energy involved in it, and your fear also has much energy, crippled and suffocated in it. If the fear disappears, the form falls away and energy is released. Anger disappears—more energy is released. Jealousy disappears—still more energy. What are called "sins" simply disappear. It is not that you have to change them; you have to love your being, and they change. Change is a by-product, a consequence; so much tremendous energy is released, you start floating higher and higher and higher. You grow wings.

Love yourself. That should be the foundational commandment. Love yourself. All else will follow, but this is the foundation.

The Other Side of Love

Fear is the other side of love. If you are in love, fear disappears. If you are not in love, fear arises—tremendous fear. Only lovers are fearless; only in a deep moment of love is there no fear. In a deep moment of love, existence becomes a home—you are not a stranger, you are not an outsider, you are accepted. Even by a single human being you are accepted, something in the depth opens—a flower-like phenomenon in the innermost being. You are accepted by someone, you are valued; you are not futile. You have a significance, a meaning.

If in your life there is no love, then you will become afraid. Then there will be fear everywhere because everywhere there are enemies, no friends, and the whole existence seems to be alien; you seem to be accidental, not rooted, not at home. Even a single human being can give you such deep at-homeness in love, what to say about being in love with the total, with the whole?

So fear, in fact, is the absence of love. And if fear is a problem for you, that shows that you are looking at the wrong side. Love should be the problem, not fear. If fear is the problem, that means you should seek love. If fear is the problem, the problem in fact is that you should be more loving so somebody can be more loving to you. You should be more open to love.

But this is the trouble: When you are in fear, you are closed. You start feeling so fearful that you stop moving toward another human being. You would like to be alone. Whenever there is somebody you feel nervous, because the other looks like an enemy. And if you are so fear-obsessed, it is a vicious circle. The absence of love creates fear in you, and now, because of fear you become closed. You become like a closed cell with no windows, because you are afraid anybody can come through the windows, and there are enemies all over. You are afraid to open the door, because when you open the door anything is possible. So even when love knocks at your door, you don't trust.

A man or a woman who is so deep-rooted in fear is always

afraid to fall in love, because then the doors of the heart will be open and the other will enter you, and the other is the enemy. Says Sartre, "The other is hell."

Lovers have known another reality: The other is heaven, the very paradise. Sartre must be living in a deep-rooted fear, anguish, anxiety. And Sartre has become very influential. In fact, he should be avoided like a disease, a dangerous disease. But he appeals to people because what he is saying, many feel the same about in their own life. That is his appeal. Depression, sadness, anguish, fear—these are Sartre's themes, the themes of the whole movement of existentialism, and people feel that these are their problems. When I talk about love, of course you feel that it is not your problem; fear is your problem. But I would like to tell you that love is your problem, not fear.

It is just like this: The house is dark and I talk about light, and you say, "You go on talking about light. It will be better if you talk about darkness, because darkness is our problem. The house is filled with darkness. Light is not our problem." But do you understand what you are saying? If darkness is your problem, talking about darkness won't help. If darkness is your problem, nothing can be done about darkness directly. You cannot throw it out, you cannot push it out, you cannot switch it off. Darkness is an absence. Nothing can be done about it directly. If you have to do anything, you have to do something with the light, not with darkness.

Pay more attention to light—how to find light, how to create light, how to enkindle a candle in the house. And then suddenly there is no darkness.

Remember: Love is the problem, never fear. You are looking at the wrong side. And you can look at the wrong side for many lives and you will not be able to solve anything. Always remember, absence should not be made a problem—because nothing can be done about it. Only presence should be made a problem, because then something can be done and it can be solved

If fear is felt, then love is the problem. Become more loving. Take few steps toward the other . . . because everybody is in fear, not only you. You wait for somebody to come to you and love you—you can wait forever because the other is also afraid. And people who are afraid become afraid of one thing absolutely, and that is being rejected.

If I go and knock at your door, the possibility is that you may reject me. That rejection will become a wound, so it is better not to go. It is better to remain alone. It is better to move on your own, not to get involved with the other because the other can reject you. The moment you approach and take initiative toward love, the first fear comes—whether the other will accept you or reject you. The possibility is there—he may reject, or she may reject.

That's why women never take a step; they are more fearful. They always wait for the man—he should come to them. They always keep the possibility of rejection or acceptance with themselves, they never give the possibility to the other because they are more afraid than men are. So many women simply wait for their whole life! Nobody comes to knock at their door, because a person who is afraid becomes, in a certain way, so closed that she puts people off. Just reaching near, and the afraid person throws such vibrations all around that anybody who is coming closer is put off. Even in their movements you can sense the fear.

Talk to a woman—if you are in a certain way feeling love and affection for her, you would like to be close. You would like to stand closer and talk. But watch the body, because body has its own language. The woman will be leaning backward, not knowingly, or she may simply back away. You are coming closer and she is backing away. Or if there is no possibility to retreat, there is a wall, then she will lean against the wall. By not leaning forward, she is telling you, "Go away." She is saying, "Don't come near me."

People sitting, people walking—watch. There are people who simply put off anybody; anybody who comes close, they become afraid. And fear is energy, just like love, a negative energy. A man who is feeling love bubbles up with a positive energy. When you come closer it is as if a magnet is attracting you; you would like to be with this person.

If fear is your problem, then think about your personality, watch it. You must have closed your doors to love, that's all. Open those doors. Of course there is the possibility of being rejected, but why be afraid? The other can only say no. A 50 percent possibility of no is there, but just because of the 50 percent possibility of no, you choose a 100 percent life of no love?

The possibility is there, but why worry? There are so many people. If one says no, don't be hurt, don't take it as a wound. Simply take it—it didn't happen. Simply take it—the other person didn't feel like moving with you; you didn't suit each other. You are different types. He has or she has not said no to *you* really; it is not personal. You didn't fit, so move ahead. And it is good that the person has said no, because if you don't fit with a person and they say yes, then you will be in real trouble. You don't realize—the other has saved you a whole life of trouble! Thank him or her and move ahead, because everybody cannot suit everybody. Every individual is so unique that in fact it is very difficult to find the right person to fit with you. In a better world, sometime in the future, people will be able to move around more, so they can go and find the right woman or the right man for themselves.

Don't be afraid of making errors, because if you are afraid of making errors you will not move at all, and you will miss the whole of life. It is better to err than not to do anything. It is better to be rejected than simply remaining with yourself, afraid and not taking any initiative—because the rejection reveals the possibility of acceptance; it is the other side of acceptance. If somebody rejects, somebody else will accept. One has to go on moving and finding the right person. When right persons meet, something clicks. They are made for each other, they fit together. Not that there will not be conflicts, not that there will not be moments of anger and fight, no. If love is alive, there will be conflict also. Sometimes there will be moments of anger also. That simply shows that love is an alive phenomenon. Sometimes sadness . . . because wherever happiness exists, sadness is bound to be there.

Only in a marriage is there no sadness, because there is no happiness either. One simply tolerates the other—it is an arrangement, it is a managed phenomenon. When you really move into life, then anger is also there—but when you love a person you accept the anger. When you love a person you accept his or her sadness also. Sometimes you go apart just to come closer again. In fact, there is a deep mechanism behind it: Lovers fight in order to fall in love again and again, so they can have small honeymoons again and again and again.

Don't be afraid of love. There is only one thing one should be afraid of, and that is fear. Be afraid of fear and never be afraid of anything else, because fear cripples. It is poisonous, it is suicidal.

Move, jump out of it! Do whatever you like, but don't get settled with the fear because that is a negative situation.

To me, love is not a great problem because I look farther ahead than you. If you miss love you will miss meditation, and that is the real problem for me. To you it may not yet be a problem, because if fear is the problem—then to you, even love is not yet a problem, how can you think about meditation? But I see the whole sequence of life and how it moves. If love is missed you can never be in meditation, because being in meditation is cosmic love. You cannot bypass love. Many people have tried, and they are dead in the monasteries. All over the world many people have tried. Because of the fear they have tried to avoid love completely, and they have been trying to find a shortcut directly from their fear to meditativeness.

That is what the monks have been doing all over the centuries, Christian and Hindu and Buddhist—all monks have been doing that. They have been trying to bypass love completely. Their prayer will be false, their prayer will have no life. Their prayer will not be heard anywhere, and the cosmos is not going to answer their prayer. They are trying to deceive the whole cosmos.

No, one has to pass through love. From fear, move into love. From love you will move into prayerfulness, meditativeness, and from meditativeness arises fearlessness. Without love fear; with love fearlessness, and the final fearlessness is in meditation because then even death is not a fear at all, then there is no death. You are so deeply in tune with existence—how can fear exist?

So please don't get obsessed with fear. Just jump out of it and take a move toward love. And don't wait, because nobody is interested in you; if you are waiting you can go on waiting.

This is my observation: You cannot bypass love; you will be committing suicide. But the love can bypass you if you are simply waiting. Move! Love should be passionate, alive, vital. Only then do you attract somebody to come toward you. Dead, who bothers with you? Dead, people would like to get rid of you. Dead, you become a boring phenomenon, a boredom. All around you, you carry such dirt of boredom that anybody who comes across you will feel that it is a misfortune to have met you.

Be loving, vital, unafraid—and move. Life has much to give to you if you are unafraid. And love has more to give you than life can give, because love is the very center of this life. And from that very center you can pass to the other shore.

I call these three steps: life, love, and light. Life is already there. Love, you have to attain. You can miss it because it is not given; one has to create it. Life is a given phenomenon; you are already alive. There, natural evolution stops. Love you have to find. Of course there are dangers, hazards, but they all make it beautiful. You have to find love, and when you find love, only then can you find light. Then the prayerfulness, meditativeness arises. It has happened to many lovers—but lovers are very rare—that while they are deep in love, suddenly they have fallen into a meditative state. Just sitting by each other's side in silence, holding each other's hand, or lying together on a beach, suddenly they have felt an urge, an urge to move beyond.

So don't pay much attention to fear, because that is dangerous. If you pay much attention to fear you are feeding it, and it will grow. Turn your back to the fear and move toward love.

5

FINDING A WAY TO
FEARLESSNESS—INSIGHTS
AND MEDITATIONS

Fear exists only in the mechanism of the mind. You will have to learn to separate yourself from the mechanism. We become so identified with the mechanism that we have completely forgotten the distance. It is just the mind, and the mind is nothing but all the conditionings that have been given to you by others.

Just start observing a little bit. For example, you see a rose flower and immediately you say, "It is beautiful." Scrutinize it, observe it: Whose words are you repeating? Is this your experience right here, now, this moment, this assertion that the flower is beautiful? Is it really your experience right now, or are you just repeating somebody's words that you heard in your childhood, or that you read in a book? A teacher, a parent, a friend . . . just remember and you will be surprised at what you find. If you look deep you will be able to find out—"Yes, it was some particular person who said for the first time—'Look, what a beautiful flower.'" That became part of your program, and since then you have been repeating it. And the more you have repeated it the more ingrained it has become. Now it is almost like a tape recording: You see the flower, the stimulus is there, and immediately the response comes and the tape starts playing. It says, "It is beautiful." It is not you who are saying that it is beautiful. You have not even been allowed to see the flower because the programming is there.

Fear is not coming from your being either. Watch it, analyze it, go into it, and you will be surprised to discover who has taught you. It is somebody in your childhood who has made you afraid of love, afraid of strangers, afraid of the unknown—hence those voices. And you will be able to find whose voices they are—your mother's, your father's . . . and I am not saying they were wrong. At the time they were made, they were relevant. But now they are irrelevant. You have grown up; now those programs don't fit. Those programs are just hangovers from the past. But they continue because the mind knows no way of erasing them—unless you become very aware, and erase them consciously.

The mind cannot erase its programs automatically. The mind only knows how to be programmed; it has no capacity to deprogram itself. That is one of the most fundamental problems to be encountered. And that's what my work consists of—helping you to become aware of the programming, so that you can begin to separate yourself and see that you are not the program. Then you will be able, when the distance is great enough, to erase many programs that have become simply out of date, which make no sense anymore but are carried and will be carried to your death if you don't separate yourself.

My own observation is that somewhere near the age of five a child becomes identified with his programmed mind. And it is only up to that time that the child is alive because he is not yet programmed. After that he becomes just a mechanism.

Around the age of five all real learning stops. One goes on repeating the program in better and better ways, more skillful, more efficient, but it is basically the same program till death . . . unless by chance you come across a situation, an energy field, where you can be made aware—almost forced against yourself to become aware of this whole nonsense that your mind is doing to you.

Whenever you encounter something new your mind says, "Wait! This is very strange—you have never done it before." The mind says, "Whatever you have not done before, don't do it; it is risky. Who knows what the outcome will be?" The mind is always orthodox because it lives through programs. It wants you to do only that which you have already been doing, because you are efficient in doing it, clever. It is safer, you know how to do it. Now moving into some strange situation—who knows what might happen? Who knows if it is right or not right? So beware! The mind says, "Follow the old program—just live the way you have lived up to now. Go on moving in the same routine and there will be less possibility of error."

The mind wants to avoid errors, and life does not want to avoid errors. It wants to go through them so that much more can be learned—because we learn only by trial and error. If we stop making errors we stop learning too. And my experience is that people who stop learning become neurotic; neurosis is a kind of nonlearning. One has become afraid of learning any more, so one goes on revolving in the same rut. One is tired, bored, but one still goes on revolving in the same rut because one has become accustomed to it; it is familiar, it is known.

When fear arises, it is simply indicative that something is going against the program that you have been carrying up to now. You have come into a situation where you will have to start learning again. That means you will have to drop your neurosis. That means that whatsoever you have done from your childhood up to now, from the age of five up to now, has to be slowly erased and dropped . . . so that you become a child again and you start from where the learning process stopped.

. . .

If you move deeply in meditation, either fear or love will become the door. If death has been suppressed, then fear will be the door. If sex has been suppressed, then love will be the door. For example, in the Eastern civilizations where sex has been suppressed, and is still suppressed, the first thing the mind faces in meditation is a deep upsurge of sex energy because in entering meditation, whatsoever is suppressed uncoils.

When you don't have any suppressions about sex, fear will uncoil. The suppressed and tabooed thing in most Western cultures is death, so you have to be deeply relaxed in allowing it. Once fear is allowed, it will soon become death; you will have to pass through a moment of death. Once sex and death are no longer taboo, a person is free.

These are the two tricks to create bondage for humanity.

Once neither of these are there, you are freedom; not that you are free—you are freedom.

NO ESCAPE

You will escape from people if you are carrying something false in you. You will not allow anybody to be friendly, to be intimate with you, because in intimacy the danger is that the other may be able to see something which strangers cannot see. You will keep people at a distance; you will run and rush away from people. You will have only formal relationships, but you will not really relate, because to really relate means to expose yourself.

Hence your so-called saints escaped into the monasteries. It was out of fear. If they were in the marketplace they would be caught; it would be discovered that they are cheating, that they are deceiving, that they are hypocrites. In the monasteries they can maintain their hypocrisy and nobody will ever be able to detect it. And moreover, there are other hypocrites there; they can all maintain their conspiracy together more easily than each single hypocrite can maintain his alone.

Monasteries came into existence for escapists. But you can live even in the world in a monastic way, keeping people always at a distance, never allowing anybody access to your inner being, never opening up, never allowing anybody to have a peek into you to see who you are, never looking into people's eyes, avoiding people's eyes, looking sideways. And always in a hurry, so that everybody knows you are so occupied, you don't have any time to say hello, to hold somebody's hand, to sit with somebody informally. You are so busy, you are always on the go.

You will not even allow intimacy with those who are close to you—husbands, wives, children—with them also you will have a formal relationship, an institutional relationship.

SELF-CONSCIOUS OR SELF-AWARE?

We have two terms that are very different but appear very similar. One is *self-consciousness,* the other is *self-awareness.* The meaning is the same as far as language is concerned, but existentially there is a great difference. Self-consciousness is a disease. The emphasis is on the self. You become self-conscious only when you are nervous, afraid. If you suddenly have to go for an interview you become self-conscious, or if you are suddenly asked to deliver a lecture standing on a podium you become self-conscious. Facing so many people who are all focusing on you creates great trembling inside.

It is said that the mind starts functioning the moment you are born till one day you stand on a podium to speak, then it stops! Then suddenly you don't know what is what. Suddenly all thoughts disappear. Those are the only moments you know of no-thought. But you miss them because you are so afraid and trembling and perspiring. That is self-consciousness. In self-consciousness, the consciousness is not important, ego is important—that's why you are trembling. You want to have a certain image; now you are afraid whether you will be able to manage it. Facing so many people you are afraid that if something goes wrong you will be exposed, that you are not so intelligent, that you are not the person that you pretend to be, that you are standing almost naked before eyes that are looking at you like X-rays. You become very concerned about the ego, how to protect your ego. That is a kind of disease.

Self-awareness is totally different. It has nothing to do with the ego. You have two selves. One is the false, the ego, which is only a belief. If you look deeply into it you will not find it anywhere. The other is your real self, your original face, your essential nature. To be aware of it is to be aware of the tremendous mystery that life is. And the only door goes through you. You cannot approach that mystery from anywhere else because the closest thing to that mystery is your own being, your own heart. You have to enter from there.

Once you have known the mystery of life through your own being, you will know it everywhere. Once you have known it within you will know it without too. But the first work has to be done in your inner world. You have to become a lab, a great experiment. You are the experiment, you are the instrument of the experiment, the lab, everything, because inside you there is nobody else, nothing else. You are all: the experimenter and the experimented upon and the experiment.

Once you start moving into the subjectivity of your inner world, of your interiority, you slowly become acquainted with the miraculous. And to be acquainted with the miraculous is to know that which is worth knowing; otherwise you just go on accumulating knowledge—which is worthless, which is simply junk.

AFRAID TO BE SILENT

People are continuously talking—yakkety-yakkety-yakkety. And the reason why they are talking is that they are afraid to be silent, they are afraid to see the truth, they are afraid to see their utter emptiness, they are afraid to expose themselves, they are afraid to look deep into the other. Continuous talking keeps them on the surface, occupied, engaged.

Holding the hand of your woman or man, why not sit silently? Why not close your eyes and feel? Feel the presence of the other, enter into the presence of the other, let the other's presence enter into you; vibrate together, sway together; if suddenly a great energy possesses you, dance together—and you will reach to such orgasmic peaks of joy as you have never known before. Those orgasmic peaks have nothing to do with sex, in fact they have much to do with silence.

And if you can also manage to become meditative in your sex life, if you can be silent while making love, in a kind of dance, you will be surprised. You have a built-in process to take you to the furthest shore.

People make love in such an ugly way that if children sometimes see their parents making love, they think they are wrestling, fighting—that Daddy is going to kill Mum! Groaning, breathing in an ugly way, violent, their movements have no elegance. It is not a dance; certainly it is not a dance.

And unless it becomes a dance it will remain just physiological; it won't have any spirituality in it. But it is impossible. Unless your whole life is saturated with those moments that come when the mind ceases, your love life cannot move into silence.

The night is full of stars. Lie down on the earth, disappear into the earth. We come from the earth, one day we will be going back to the earth to rest forever. At night sometimes, lying on the lawn, disappear into the earth. Look at the stars—just look, a pure look. Don't start thinking about the names of the stars, the names of the constellations. Forget all that you know about stars, put aside all your knowledge, just see the stars. And suddenly there will be a communion; the stars will start pouring their light into you, and you will feel an expanding of consciousness. No drug can do it.

Drugs are very artificial, arbitrary, and harmful methods to know something which is naturally available, which is easily available, beneficially available. Just watching the stars, you will start feeling high, you will start soaring high.

Make as much as you can of all the opportunities that life and existence allow you. Never miss a single opportunity when you can drop the mind, and slowly, slowly you will know the knack of it. It is a knack—it is certainly not a science, because it has no fixed methods.

Somebody may be thrilled by the stars, somebody may not be. Somebody may be thrilled by the flowers, somebody else may not be affected at all. People are so different that there is no way of determining it in a scientific way; it is not a science. It is not even an art, because an art can be taught.

So I insist on the word *knack*. It is a knack. You have to learn it by doing a few experiments with yourself.

WHATEVER FRIGHTENS YOU, GO INTO IT

Whatever frightens you, go into it. Just put aside all safety measures, securities; just gamble. The whole of life belongs to the gambler, and the whole mind has become a businessman: calculating, thinking of profit and loss, never taking a risk—and risk is needed. Life comes to those who risk, who live dangerously, almost on the verge of death.

That was the attraction in the past of being a soldier, a warrior. The attraction was not of war, but of danger—just to move side-by-side with death. It gives you a crystallization, and there comes a time when no fear remains in you.

Just imagine a point where no fear is in you. That is freedom, what Hindus call *moksha*—absolute freedom. Fear is the bondage. There is no other bondage than fear. Fear is the imprisonment. Nobody is imprisoning you . . . it is your own fear, and you go on hiding yourself behind the walls. You have become crippled and you cannot come out in the open. Your eyes have become blind because you have lived so much in darkness, so whenever you come against light it is too dazzling.

Whenever you come near fear, you are near the door. Fear is symbolic. It says now be aware, don't enter here; death is here. But death is the door—to enlightenment, to all that is beautiful and true. Learn to die; that is the only way to achieve more and more abundant life.

Life arises only in risk, in danger. When danger is there, all around you, something in you crystallizes, because that danger changes you. The danger creates a situation in which you have to become one. You cannot go on thinking; you become thoughtless.

Have you watched that when you suddenly come across a snake on the road, thinking stops? Immediately there is no thought— the mind is vacant because the situation is so dangerous that you cannot afford to think. Thinking will take time, and the snake is there and may not wait for you . . . he may strike.

So you have to do something without thinking. You have to move with no mind, you jump—not that you decide to jump; you jump without any decision on the part of the mind. After you have taken the jump the mind comes back and you start thinking about many things. You may forget that the jump happened out of meditation, that it was spontaneous.

Whenever there is danger, thinking stops. Thinking is a luxury. When people become too secure, they think too much—noise of no value, much ado about nothing. This inner talk becomes a barrier on every sense—it becomes like a dead weight. It does not allow you to see, it does not allow you to hear, it does not allow you to live, it does not allow you to love. Fear kills people before death comes. A man dies a thousand and one times before death comes. Real death is beautiful, but the death that fear projects is the ugliest thing.

So next time make this the key: Whenever fear arises, that means you are somewhere near the block that has to be broken—just there, somewhere near the door. Knock hard and enter there. Be a fool and enter. Don't try to be clever—be a fool, and much is possible.

BEWARE OF THE TWO EXTREMES

These two things have to be remembered; these are the two extremes. Either people start repressing their fear and start trying to impose some bravery, courage—which is going to be false because deep underneath there will be fear—or people become so afraid that they become paralyzed; then the fear becomes a hindrance. In both ways you will be stuck with fear. The right way is to accept it so that there is no need to repress. Accept its naturalness—that is natural, bound to be so. Accept the fact of it and still go ahead, bypass it. Don't repress it and don't be hindered by it. In spite of it, go on moving. Trembling, of course, because the fear is there, but go on moving. Trembling, but go on rushing toward the abyss.

Don't impose fearlessness, because an imposed fearlessness is a pseudo thing, a counterfeit. It has no value. So just be natural, authentic, sincere. Take note that the fear exists, but still go on. That's what I mean when I say go in spite of the fear. Trembling, okay; shaking, okay—go on! Tremble like a small new leaf in the strong wind.

Have you seen the strength of a new leaf? So fragile, so weak, and yet so strong. Even when the storm is raging, the leaf goes on trembling—but have you seen its beauty? The fear is there, because fear is always there when something is alive. Only in a dead thing is there no fear. The fear is there, the storm is raging, and the leaf is small and delicate, tender, soft. It can be crushed very easily, but have you seen its strength? Still it goes on dancing, singing. Still it goes on trusting in life.

So be soft, be tender, be delicate, be afraid, but never be hindered by it and don't repress it. Accept the limitations, the human limitations, but still go on working beyond them. That's how one grows.

DON'T BE IN A HURRY

Fear can be dissolved, but don't be in a hurry to get rid of it; otherwise you will repress it. Be patient, watch it, try to understand it. Accept it as part of you. Don't say that it is something ugly that is clinging to you—that is rejecting it, and rejecting it will not help. It is just a part of you. Just as love is a part, so is fear; it is part of you just as anger is.

Never reject any emotion, because all those emotions constitute you, and they are all needed. Of course no single emotion should become an obsession; they should be a kind of orchestra within you, they should remain in a proportionate way. No one single emotion should overwhelm you, that's all that has to be remembered. But no emotion should be rejected in toto.

Fear has its own place—it is needed, without it you will lose something—but it should not become a phobia. One has to keep balance.

There are people who are so full of fear that fear spreads all over their being; that is pathological. And there are people who are so afraid of fear that they repress it, they condemn it, they reject it so totally that they become almost like rocks. That too is pathological. Fear has its own place in the inner economy, it has something to contribute of immense importance.

Sometimes in your life the fear may be a little too much, but don't go to the other extreme and reject it completely. It has to be brought in to a normal harmony with other emotions; it has to remain there.

So first, drop the idea of dropping fear. Second, accept it; it is part of you. And third, watch it, observe it; try to understand why it is there and what it is. If you do these three things you will bring it into balance. Your fear will not disappear, but it will not be too much either. It will be exactly as much as is needed by you.

DON'T MAKE FEARLESSNESS A GOAL

A goal is the trick of the mind to create misery. Create a goal and then you are miserable because then anxiety arises: How to achieve it? I have not achieved it yet. You go on searching and searching and you never achieve it. You remain miserable and you go on missing all the joys of life because your eyes are focused on the future. You are here, and your eyes are focused on the future.

Try to understand this: The body exists here, but the mind is not here. That is the dichotomy, that is the problem. When you drink water the body drinks here and now. The body cannot drink water in the future, it cannot drink water in the past, because the past is no more, the future is not yet. When you feel hungry, you feel hungry here and now. And I am not talking about the hunger that the mind can create; I am talking about the bodily hunger. The body is always in the present and the mind is never in the present, never; hence anxiety is created, and the feeling that one is being torn apart. The mind goes on rushing toward the future and the body is here. Then the mind starts condemning the body as if the body is lethargic, slow, cannot keep pace.

The body is simply here, not lethargic. And the mind has to learn one thing—to come back to the body. Get out of your mind and into your senses and you will also have that confidence, that joy. No god is needed to give you joy, no truth is needed to give you joy and significance. All that is needed is that your body and mind have to be bridged; it is a simple process. And don't make this bridging a goal. If you make it a goal, again the same problem has come in from the back door.

Just understand! Then suddenly you have all your energy available; you are confident, you are happy and you start moving with no fear. Not that insecurity disappears; insecurity remains. That is part of life, it is inbuilt. Those people who think they are secure are simply fools; nobody can ever be secure while they are alive. You will only be secure when you are in your grave, never before that. How can you be secure? Illness is there, death is there, the friend may die, the beloved may go somewhere else. How can you be secure? The bank may fail, you may go bankrupt, your job may be lost, you may lose your eyesight, you may become crippled, paralyzed. A thousand and one things are all around; how can you be secure?

But the very idea to become secure creates the trouble. I help people to start enjoying insecurity. Not that I make them secure; how can I? Nobody can do that and it is not good to do it either. Even if somebody could do it, it should not be done because when a man is secure he is dead; then you cannot live.

Life comes with death. When you breathe in, you will have to breathe out; you cannot say, "I will only breathe in." They come together—breathing in, breathing out. Life is breathing in, death is breathing out. Love is breathing in, hate is breathing out. Joy is breathing in, sadness is breathing out. Marriage is breathing in, divorce is breathing out; they come together!

Now, if you want marriage without divorce, the marriage will be plastic; it will not have any joy. You will be secure but there will be no joy, because how can you be happy with a dead thing? If you want your wife to be alive, then there is risk. An alive woman is a dangerous woman; she may fall in love again, who knows? An alive person is an alive person; love can happen again! If you are alive you can fall in love with other women. Life knows no laws, no moralities.

Only death can be controlled—so the more dead you are, the more easily you can be controlled. Then you remain a husband or a wife and this and that, and things at least look secure. A middle-class home, a bank balance, a car in the garage, a woman, a man, children, a good job, and one feels that one is secure. But is this security? Security is not possible; only comforts are possible. These are comforts, not security—and they can be taken back, they can be taken away.

The only security possible is to start enjoying insecurity. That looks paradoxical, but all that is true in life is always paradoxical. Truth is a paradox. Love insecurity and it disappears. Not that you become secure, but when you start loving and enjoying insecurity, who bothers? There is no worry, no anxiety about it. One is really thrilled. One is thrilled; one wonders what tomorrow is going to bring. And one remains open.

AFRAID TO EXHALE

Death and life are two polarities of the same energy, of the same phenomenon—the tide and the ebb, the day and the night, the summer and the winter. They are not separate and not opposites, not contrary; they are complementary. Death is not the end of life; in fact, it is a completion of one life, the crescendo of one life, the climax, the finale. And once you know your life and its process, then you understand what death is.

Death is an organic, integral part of life, and it is very friendly to life. Without it life cannot exist. Life exists because of death; death gives the background. Death is, in fact, a process of renewal. And death happens each moment. The moment you breathe in and the moment you breathe out, both happen. Breathing in, life happens; breathing out, death happens. That's why when a child is born the first thing he does is breathe in, then life starts. And when an old man is dying, the last thing he does is breathe out, then life departs. Breathing out is death, breathing in is life—they are like two wheels of a bullock cart. You live by breathing in as much as you live by breathing out. The breathing out is part of breathing in. You cannot breathe in if you stop breathing out. You cannot live if you stop dying. One who has understood what his life is allows death to happen; he welcomes it. He dies each moment and each moment he is resurrected. His cross and his resurrection are continually happening as a process. He dies to the past each moment and he is born again and again into the future.

If you look into life you will be able to know what death is. If you understand what death is, only then are you able to understand what life is. They are organic. Ordinarily, out of fear, we have created a division. We think that life is good and death is bad. We think that life has to be desired and death is to be avoided. We think somehow we have to protect ourselves against death. This absurd idea creates endless miseries in our lives, because a person who protects himself against death becomes incapable of living. He is the person who is afraid of exhaling, then he cannot inhale and he is stuck. Then he simply drags; his life is no longer a flow, his life is no longer a river.

If you really want to live you have to be ready to die. Who is afraid of death in you? Is life afraid of death? It is not possible. How can life be afraid of its own integral process? Something else is afraid in you. The ego is afraid in you. Life and death are not opposites; ego and death are opposites. Life and death are not opposites; ego and life are opposites. Ego is against both life and death. The ego is afraid to live and the ego is afraid to die. It is afraid to live because each effort, each step toward life, brings death closer.

If you live you are coming closer to dying. The ego is afraid to die, hence it is afraid to live also. The ego simply drags.

There are many people who are neither alive nor dead. This is worse than anything. A man who is fully alive is full of death also. That is the meaning of Jesus on the cross. Jesus carrying his own cross has not really been understood. And he says to his disciples, "You will have to carry your own cross." The meaning of Jesus carrying his own cross is very simple, nothing but this: Everybody has to carry his death continuously, everybody has to die each moment, everybody has to be on the cross because that is the only way to live fully, totally.

Whenever you come to a total moment of aliveness, suddenly you will see death there also. In love it happens. In love, life comes to a climax—hence people are afraid of love.

I have been continuously surprised by people who come to me and say they are afraid of love. What is the fear of love? It is because when you really love somebody your ego starts slipping and melting. You cannot love with the ego; the ego becomes a barrier. And when you want to drop the barrier the ego says, "This is going to be a death. Beware!"

The death of the ego is not your death. The death of the ego is really your possibility of life. The ego is just a dead crust around you, it has to be broken and thrown away. It comes into being naturally—just as when a traveler passes, dust collects on his clothes, on his body, and he has to take a bath to get rid of the dust.

As we move in time, dust of experiences, of knowledge, of lived life, of past, collects. That dust becomes our ego. Accumulated, it becomes a crust around you which has to be broken and thrown away. One has to take a bath continuously—every day, in fact every moment, so that this crust never becomes a prison.

IF FEAR IS THERE, ACCEPT IT

If there is fear and you start *doing* something about it, then a new fear has entered: Fear of the fear; it has become more complex. So if fear is there, accept it. Don't *do* anything about it because "doing" will not help. Anything that you do out of fear will create more fear; anything that you do out of confusion will add more confusion. Don't do anything! If fear is there, note that fear is there and accept it. What can you do? Nothing can be done.

"Fear is there." See? If you can just note down the fact that fear is there, where is the fear? You have accepted it; it has dissolved. Acceptance dissolves it—only acceptance, nothing else. If you fight with it you create another disturbance, and this can go on ad infinitum; then there is no end to it.

People come to me and they say, "We are very afraid, what should we do?" If I give them something to do they will do it with the being which is full of fear, so their action will come out of their fear. And the action that comes out of fear cannot be anything other than fearful.

If you have one problem, don't create another. Remain with the first one, don't fight with it and create another. It is easier to solve the first problem than to solve a second, and the first is nearer to the source. The second will be removed from the source, and the further removed the more impossible it becomes to solve it.

If you have fear, you have fear—why make a problem out of it? Then you know that you have fear, just as you have two hands. Why create a problem out of it, as if you have only one nose and not two? Why create a problem out of it? Fear is there—accept it, note it. Accept it and don't bother about it. What will happen? Suddenly you will feel it has disappeared.

This is the inner alchemy: A problem disappears if you accept it, and a problem grows more and more complex if you create any conflict with it. Yes, suffering is there, and suddenly fear comes—accept it; it is there, and nothing can be done about it. And when I say nothing can be done about it, don't think that I am talking about pessimism. When I say nothing can be done about it I am giving you a key to solve it.

Suffering is there—it is part of life and part of growth, nothing is bad in it. Suffering becomes evil only when it is simply destructive and not creative at all; suffering becomes bad only when you suffer and nothing is gained from it. But I am telling you that insight can be gained through suffering and then it becomes creative.

Darkness is beautiful if the dawn is coming out of it soon; darkness is dangerous if it is endless, leads to no dawn, simply continues and continues and you go on moving in a rut, in a vicious circle. This can happen if you are not alert—just to escape from one suffering you can create another; then to escape from another, yet another. And this goes on and on, and all those sufferings that you have not lived are still waiting for you. You have escaped, but you simply escaped from one suffering to another—because the same mind that was creating a suffering will create another. You can escape from this suffering to that, but suffering will still be there because your mind is the creative force.

Accept suffering and pass through it; don't escape. This is a totally different dimension to work in. Suffering is there—encounter it, go through it. Fear will be there—accept it. You will tremble—so tremble! Why pretend that you don't tremble, that you are not afraid? If you are a coward, accept it.

Everyone is a coward. People you call brave are just pretending. Deep down they are as cowardly as anyone else; in fact *more* cowardly because just to hide that cowardliness they have created a brave face and are trying to act in such a way that everyone thinks they are not cowards. Their bravery is just a screen.

How can we be brave? Death is there. How can we be brave—because each of us is just a leaf in the wind. How can the leaf not tremble? When the wind blows, the leaf will tremble. But you never say to the leaf, "You are a coward." You only say that the leaf is alive. So when you tremble and fear takes hold of you, you are a leaf in the wind—beautiful! Why create a problem out of it? But society has made a problem out of everything.

If a child is afraid in the dark, we say, "Don't be afraid, be brave." Why? The child is innocent; naturally he feels fear in the dark. You force him—"Be brave!"—so he also forces himself. Then he becomes tense. Then he endures the darkness but now he is tense; now his whole being is ready to tremble and he suppresses it. This suppressed trembling will follow him his whole life. It would have been all right to tremble in the darkness, nothing is wrong in it. It would have been good to cry and run to his mother and father, nothing is wrong in it. The child would have come out of the darkness more experienced, more knowing. He would have realized, if he passed through the darkness trembling and crying and weeping, that there was nothing to fear. Suppressed, you never experience the thing in its totality; you never gain anything out of it.

Wisdom comes through suffering and wisdom comes through acceptance. Whatsoever the case, be at ease with it. Don't take any notice of the society and its condemnation. Nobody has the right to judge you and nobody can pretend to be a judge. Don't judge others, and don't be perturbed and disturbed by others' judgment. You are alone and you are unique. You never were before, you never will be again. You are beautiful! Accept it, and whatsoever happens, allow it to happen and pass through it. Soon, suffering will become learning; then it has become creative.

Fear will give you fearlessness, out of anger will come compassion. Out of the understanding of hate, love will be born to you. But this happens not in a conflict, this happens in a passing-through with alert awareness. Accept, and pass through it.

NOTHING TO LOSE

There is nothing to fear because we don't have anything to lose. Nobody can rob us, and all that can be robbed is not worthwhile, so why fear, why suspect, why doubt? These are the real robbers—doubt, suspicion, fear. They destroy your very possibility of celebration.

So while on earth, celebrate the earth. While this moment lasts, enjoy it to the very core. Take all the juice that it can give to you and is ready to give to you.

Because of fear you miss many things. Because of fear we cannot love, or even if we love it is always halfhearted, it is always so-so. It is always up to a certain extent and not beyond that. We always come to a point beyond which we are afraid, so we are stuck there. We cannot move deep in friendship because of fear. We cannot be prayerful because of fear.

There are people who go on saying that people pray because of fear. That's true; many people pray because of fear. But there is an even greater truth, which is that many people don't go the whole way in prayer because of fear. They may start in fear but then they don't go very far. They just remain on a formal, clichéd level. They say some formal prayer but they really are not moved, thrilled by it; it is not an ecstasy. They are not mad with it, they don't go headlong. They move very cautiously—and all caution is based in fear.

Be conscious, but never be cautious. The distinction is very subtle. Consciousness is not rooted in fear, caution is rooted in fear. One is cautious so that one may never go wrong, but then one cannot go very far. The very fear will not allow you to investigate new lifestyles, new channels of energy, new directions, new lands; it will not allow you. You will always tread on the same path again and again, shuttling backward and forward, shuttling backward and forward. One becomes like a freight train.

Consciousness simply says, "Be conscious of whatsoever you are doing, wherever you are going. Just remain alert so you can enjoy it to the very last drop, so nothing is missed, you are alert."

Fear is one of the most basic problems to be faced, encountered. So if you feel your fear is growing less, make it even lesser. It is like weeds in the garden; one has to go on continually pulling them up and throwing them away, otherwise they tend to overrun the whole garden. If you allow the weeds, sooner or later the roses will disappear, flowers will disappear and there will be weeds all over the garden. One has to go on continually pulling them up. Only then can the garden remain beautiful. When all the roots are uprooted, then there is no problem. You can relax.

This is the whole effort, the very inner discipline, the work.

Gurdjieff used to say to his disciples, "Find your chief characteristic," because around that everything is hooked. For example, one has a guilt feeling; that is the person's chief characteristic and everything is hooked around it. If you lose the guilt feeling then everything else will drop by itself. And for another type of person, if he drops his fear there is nothing else to drop. Everything else will drop automatically because everything else is just an outgrowth of the fear.

Wherever you see that there is fear, drop it. And sometimes if it is needed, then go into the fear. In life there is nothing which is bad, nothing which has to be feared—nothing whatsoever. It is just that we have certain ideas implanted in the mind, in certain fragile moments, and they go on projecting. A small child is left in the crib. He is hungry and he cries out, looks around and he cannot see anything; it is dark and nobody is coming. Now the aloneness, the hunger, nobody responding to his call and cry, and the fear, all become associated. They become associated so deeply that whenever he is in the dark, even after fifty years, he will start feeling a certain fear. That fifty-year-old association is still alive. Now he is no longer a child, no longer in the crib, no longer dependent on the mother, but still that fear is there functioning and projecting.

So just watch and drop fear more and more. If you can clean your consciousness of fear you have come to the right path. Then the real journey of celebration starts.

JOY IS THE ANTIDOTE

Joy is the antidote for all fear. Fear comes if you don't enjoy life. If you enjoy life, fear disappears. So just be positive and enjoy more, laugh more, dance more, sing. Remain more and more cheerful, enthusiastic about small things, very small things. Life consists of small things, but if you can bring the quality of cheerfulness to small things, the total is tremendous.

Don't wait for anything great to happen. Great things happen, it is not that they don't, but don't wait for the something great to happen. It happens only when you start living small, ordinary, day-to-day things with a new mind, with new freshness, with new vitality, with new enthusiasm. Then by and by you accumulate, and that accumulation one day explodes into sheer joy.

But one never knows when it will happen. One has just to go on collecting pebbles on the shore. The totality becomes the great happening. When you collect one pebble, it is a pebble. When all the pebbles are together, suddenly they are diamonds. That's the miracle of life. So you need not think about these great things.

There are many people in the world who miss because they are always waiting for something great. It can't happen. It happens only through small things: eating, taking your breakfast, walking, taking your bath, talking to a friend, just sitting alone looking at the sky, or lying on your bed doing nothing. These small things are what life is made of. This is the very stuff of life.

So do everything cheerfully and then everything becomes a prayer.

Do it with enthusiasm. The word *enthusiasm* is very beautiful. The basic root means *god-given*. When you do something with deep enthusiasm, godliness is within you. The very word *enthusiasm* means one who is full of godliness. So just bring more enthusiasm into life, and fear and other things will disappear on their own.

Never be bothered by negatives. You burn the candle and the darkness goes on its own. Don't try to fight with the darkness. There is no way, because the darkness does not exist. How can you fight with it? Just light a candle and the darkness is gone. So forget about the darkness, forget about the fear. Forget about all those negative things that ordinarily haunt the human mind. Just burn a small candle of enthusiasm.

For fifteen days, the first thing in the morning, get up with a great enthusiasm—"godliness within"—with a decision that today you are going to really live with great delight. And then start living with great delight! Have your breakfast, but eat it as if you are eating god himself; it becomes a sacrament. Take your bath, but godliness is within you; you are giving a bath to god. Then your small bathroom becomes a temple and the water showering on you is a baptism.

Get up every morning with a great decision, a certainty, a clarity, a promise to yourself that today is going to be tremendously beautiful and you are going to live it tremendously. And each night when you go to bed, remember again how many beautiful things have happened today. Just the remembrance helps them to come back again tomorrow. Just remember and then fall asleep remembering those beautiful moments that happened today. Your dreams will be more beautiful. They will carry your enthusiasm, your totality, and you will start living in dreams also, with a new energy.

OSHO INTERNATIONAL
MEDITATION RESORT

Location: Located 100 miles southeast of Mumbai in the thriving modern city of Pune, India, the OSHO International Meditation Resort is a holiday destination with a difference. The Meditation Resort is spread over 40 acres of spectacular gardens in a gorgeous tree-lined residential area.

Uniqueness: Each year the meditation resort welcomes thousands of people from more than 100 countries. The unique campus provides an opportunity for a direct personal experience of a new way of living—with more awareness, relaxation, celebration, and creativity. A great variety of around-the-clock and around-the-year program options are available. Doing nothing and just relaxing is one of them!

All programs are based on the OSHO vision of "Zorba the Buddha"—a qualitatively new kind of human being who is able *both* to participate creatively in everyday life *and* to relax into silence and meditation.

Meditations: A full daily schedule of meditations for every type of person includes methods that are active and passive, traditional and revolutionary, and in particular the OSHO Active Meditations™. The meditations take place in what must be the world's largest meditation hall, the Osho Auditorium.

Multiversity: Individual sessions, courses, and workshops cover everything from creative arts to holistic health, personal transformation, relationship and life transition, work-as-meditation, esoteric sciences, and the "Zen" approach to sports and recreation. The secret of the Multiversity's success lies in the fact that all its programs are combined with meditation, supporting an understanding that as human beings we are far more than the sum of our parts.

Basho Spa: The luxurious Basho Spa provides for leisurely open-air swimming surrounded by trees and tropical green. The uniquely styled, spacious Jacuzzi, the saunas, gym, tennis courts . . . all are enhanced by their stunningly beautiful setting.

Cuisine: A variety of different eating areas serve delicious Western, Asian, and Indian vegetarian food—most of it organically grown especially for the meditation resort. Breads and cakes are baked in the resort's own bakery.

Nightlife: There are many evening events to choose from—dancing being at the top of the list! Other activities include full-moon meditations beneath the stars, variety shows, music performances, and meditations for daily life.

Or you can just enjoy meeting people at the Plaza Café, or walking in the nighttime serenity of the gardens of this fairy-tale environment.

Facilities: You can buy all your basic necessities and toiletries in the Galleria. The Multimedia Gallery sells a large range of OSHO media products. There is also a bank, a travel agency, and a Cyber Café on-campus. For those who enjoy shopping, Pune provides all options, ranging from traditional and ethnic Indian products to all global brand-name stores.

OSHO INTERNATIONAL RESORT • 171

Accommodation: You can choose to stay in the elegant rooms of the Osho Guesthouse, or for longer stays opt for one of the Living-In program packages. Additionally there is a plentiful variety of nearby hotels and serviced apartments.

www.osho.com/meditationresort

ABOUT OSHO

Osho defies categorization. His thousands of talks cover everything from the individual quest for meaning to the most urgent social and political issues facing society today. Osho's books are not written but are transcribed from audio and video recordings of his extemporaneous talks to international audiences. As he put it, "So remember: Whatever I am saying is not just for you . . . I am talking also for the future generations."

Osho has been described by the *Sunday Times* in London as one of the "one thousand makers of the twentieth century" and by American author Tom Robbins as "the most dangerous man since Jesus Christ." *Sunday Mid-Day* (India) has selected Osho as one of ten people—along with Gandhi, Nehru, and Buddha—who have changed the destiny of India.

About his own work Osho has said that he is helping to create the conditions for the birth of a new kind of human being. He often characterizes this new human being as "Zorba the Buddha" —capable both of enjoying the earthly pleasures of a Zorba the Greek and the silent serenity of a Gautam Buddha.

Running like a thread through all aspects of Osho's talks and meditations is a vision that encompasses both the timeless wisdom of all ages past and the highest potential of today's (and tomorrow's) science and technology.

Osho is known for his revolutionary contribution to the science of inner transformation, with an approach to meditation that acknowledges the accelerated pace of contemporary life. His unique OSHO Active Meditations are designed to first release the accumulated stresses of body and mind, so that it is then easier to take an experience of stillness and thought-free relaxation into daily life.

Two autobiographical works by the author are available:
Autobiography of a Spiritually Incorrect Mystic
Glimpses of a Golden Childhood

FOR MORE INFORMATION

www.OSHO.com

A comprehensive multilanguage Web site including a magazine, OSHO Books, OSHO TALKS in audio and video formats, the OSHO Library text archive in English and Hindi and extensive information about OSHO Meditations. You will also find the program schedule of the OSHO Multiversity and information about the OSHO International Meditation Resort.

Web site :
   www.OSHO.com.resort
   www.OSHO.com/allaboutOSHO
   www.OSHO.com/magazine
   www.OSHO.com/shop
   www.youtube.com/OSHO
   www.oshobytes.blogspot.com
   www.Twitter.com/OSHO
   www.facebook.com/pages/OSHO.International
   www.flickr.com/photos/oshointernational

To contact **OSHO International Foundation:**
www.osho.com/oshointernational
oshointernational@oshointernational.com

LIFE, LOVE, LAUGHTER:
CELEBRATING YOUR EXISTENCE

In this collection of reflections, Osho's inspiring and loving stories go far beyond the usual chicken-soup fare. Osho mixes entertainment and inspiration, ancient Zen stories and contemporary jokes to help us find love, laughter, and ultimately, happiness. An original talk by Osho on DVD is included.

ISBN: 978-0-312-53109-6 • Paperback w/DVD
$14.95/$18.95 Can.

LOVE, FREEDOM, ALONENESS:
THE KOAN OF RELATIONSHIPS

Love can only happen through freedom and in conjunction with a deep respect for ourselves and the other. Is it possible to be alone and not lonely? Where are the boundaries that define "lust" versus "love" and can lust ever grow into love? Osho offers unique, radical, and intelligent perspectives on these and other essential questions, as well as a golden opportunity to start afresh with ourselves, our relationships to others, and to find fulfillment and success for the individual and for society as a whole.

ISBN: 978-0-312-29162-4 • Paperback • $15.99/$18.50 Can.

OSHO INSIGHTS FOR
A NEW WAY OF LIVING SERIES

The Insights for a New Way of Living series aims to shine light on beliefs and attitudes that prevent individuals from being their true selves. Each book is an artful mixture of compassion and humor, and readers are encouraged to confront what they would most like to avoid, which in turn provides the key to true insight and power.

978-0-312-53857-6

978-0-312-20517-1

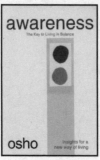

978-0-312-27563-1

978-0-312-27566-2

978-0-312-20519-5

978-0-312-36568-4

Please visit **www.stmartins.com/osho** for additional information on these titles, as well as *FREEDOM, INTELLIGENCE, INTUITION,* and *MATURITY.*

 TAKE A NEW LOOK   www.OSHO.com

ST. MARTIN'S GRIFFIN

OSHO LIFE ESSENTIALS

The Osho Life Essentials series focuses on the most important questions in the life of the individual. Each volume contains timeless and always contemporary investigations into and discussions of questions vital to our personal search for meaning and purpose.

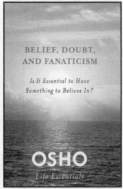

BELIEF, DOUBT, AND FANATICISM

Is It Essential to Have Something to Believe In?

OSHO *Life Essentials*

978-0-312-59548-7

THE JOURNEY OF BEING HUMAN

Is It Possible to Find Real Happiness in Ordinary Life?

OSHO *Life Essentials*

978-0-312-59547-0

DESTINY, FREEDOM, AND THE SOUL

What Is the Meaning of Life?

OSHO *Life Essentials*

978-0-312-59543-2

FAME, FORTUNE, AND AMBITION

What Is the Real Meaning of Success?

OSHO *Life Essentials*

978-0-312-59544-9

INNOCENCE, KNOWLEDGE, AND WONDER

What Happened to the Sense of Wonder I Felt as a Child?

OSHO *Life Essentials*

978-0-312-59545-6

POWER, POLITICS, AND CHANGE

What Can I Do to Help Make the World a Better Place?

OSHO *Life Essentials*

978-0-312-59546-3

Please visit www.osho.com or www.stmartins.com/osho
for additional information on these titles.

 ST. MARTIN'S GRIFFIN